# AWS WAF, AWS Firewall Manager, and AWS Shield Advanced Developer Guide

A catalogue record for this book is available from the Hong Kong Public Libraries.

Published in Hong Kong by Samurai Media Limited.

Email: info@samuraimedia.org

ISBN 9789888407866

# Contents

# What Are AWS WAF, AWS Shield, and AWS Firewall Manager?

AWS WAF is a web application firewall that lets you monitor the HTTP and HTTPS requests that are forwarded to Amazon CloudFront or an Application Load Balancer. AWS WAF also lets you control access to your content. Based on conditions that you specify, such as the IP addresses that requests originate from or the values of query strings, CloudFront or an Application Load Balancer responds to requests either with the requested content or with an HTTP 403 status code (Forbidden). You also can configure CloudFront to return a custom error page when a request is blocked.

At the simplest level, AWS WAF lets you choose one of the following behaviors:

- **Allow all requests except the ones that you specify** – This is useful when you want CloudFront or an Application Load Balancer to serve content for a public website, but you also want to block requests from attackers.
- **Block all requests except the ones that you specify** – This is useful when you want to serve content for a restricted website whose users are readily identifiable by properties in web requests, such as the IP addresses that they use to browse to the website.
- **Count the requests that match the properties that you specify** – When you want to allow or block requests based on new properties in web requests, you first can configure AWS WAF to count the requests that match those properties without allowing or blocking those requests. This lets you confirm that you didn't accidentally configure AWS WAF to block all the traffic to your website. When you're confident that you specified the correct properties, you can change the behavior to allow or block requests.

Using AWS WAF has several benefits:

- Additional protection against web attacks using conditions that you specify. You can define conditions by using characteristics of web requests such as the following:
  - IP addresses that requests originate from.
  - Country that requests originate from.
  - Values in request headers.
  - Strings that appear in requests, either specific strings or string that match regular expression (regex) patterns.
  - Length of requests.
  - Presence of SQL code that is likely to be malicious (known as *SQL injection*).
  - Presence of a script that is likely to be malicious (known as *cross-site scripting*).
- Rules that can allow, block, or count web requests that meet the specified conditions. Alternatively, rules can block or count web requests that not only meet the specified conditions, but also exceed a specified number of requests in any 5-minute period.
- Rules that you can reuse for multiple web applications.
- Real-time metrics and sampled web requests.
- Automated administration using the AWS WAF API.

## AWS Shield

You can use AWS WAF web access control lists (web ACLs) to help minimize the effects of a distributed denial of service (DDoS) attack. For additional protection against DDoS attacks, AWS also provides AWS Shield Standard and AWS Shield Advanced. AWS Shield Standard is automatically included at no extra cost beyond what you already pay for AWS WAF and your other AWS services. AWS Shield Advanced provides expanded DDoS attack protection for your Amazon EC2 instances, Elastic Load Balancing load balancers, CloudFront distributions, and Route 53 hosted zones. AWS Shield Advanced incurs additional charges.

For more information about AWS Shield Standard and AWS Shield Advanced, see AWS Shield.

# AWS Firewall Manager

AWS Firewall Manager simplifies your AWS WAF administration and maintenance tasks across multiple accounts and resources. With Firewall Manager, you set up your firewall rules just once. The service automatically applies your rules across your accounts and resources, even as you add new resources.

For more information about Firewall Manager, see AWS Firewall Manager.

# Which Should I Choose?

You can use AWS WAF, AWS Firewall Manager, and AWS Shield together to create a comprehensive security solution.

It all starts with AWS WAF. You can automate and then simplify AWS WAF management using AWS Firewall Manager. Shield Advanced adds additional features on top of AWS WAF, such as dedicated support from the DDoS Response Team (DRT) and advanced reporting.

If you want granular control over the protection that is added to your resources, AWS WAF alone is the right choice. If you want to use AWS WAF across accounts, accelerate your AWS WAF configuration, or automate protection of new resources, use Firewall Manager with AWS WAF.

Finally, if you own high visibility websites or are otherwise prone to frequent DDoS attacks, you should consider purchasing the additional features that Shield Advanced provides.

# Setting Up

This topic describes preliminary steps, such as creating an AWS account, to prepare you to use AWS WAF, AWS Firewall Manager, and AWS Shield Advanced. You are not charged to set up this account and other preliminary items. You are charged only for AWS services that you use.

After you complete these steps, see Getting Started with AWS WAF to continue getting started with AWS WAF.

**Note**
AWS Shield Standard is included with AWS WAF and does not require additional setup. For more information, see How AWS Shield Works.

Before you use AWS WAF or AWS Shield Advanced for the first time, complete the following tasks:

- Step 1: Sign Up for an AWS Account
- Step 2: Create an IAM User
- Step 3: Download Tools

## Step 1: Sign Up for an AWS Account

When you sign up for Amazon Web Services (AWS), your AWS account is automatically signed up for all services in AWS, including AWS WAF. You are charged only for the services that you use.

If you have an AWS account already, skip to the next task. If you don't have an AWS account, use the following procedure to create one.

**To sign up for AWS**

1. Open https://aws.amazon.com/ and choose **Sign Up**.

2. Follow the on-page instructions.

   Part of the sign-up procedure involves receiving a phone call and entering a PIN using the phone keypad.

Note your AWS account number, because you'll need it for the next task.

## Step 2: Create an IAM User

To use the AWS WAF console, you must sign in to confirm that you have permission to perform AWS WAF operations. You can use the root credentials for your AWS account, but we don't recommend it. For greater security and control of your account, we recommend that you use AWS Identity and Access Management (IAM) to do the following:

- Create an IAM user account for yourself or your business.
- Either add the IAM user account to an IAM group that has administrative permissions, or grant administrative permissions directly to the IAM user account.

You then can sign in to the AWS WAF console (and other service consoles) by using a special URL and the credentials for the IAM user. You also can add other users to the IAM user account, and control their level of access to AWS services and to your resources.

**Note**
For information about creating access keys to access AWS WAF by using the AWS Command Line Interface (AWS CLI), Tools for Windows PowerShell, the AWS SDKs, or the AWS WAF API, see Managing Access Keys for IAM Users.

If you signed up for AWS but have not created an IAM user for yourself, you can create one using the IAM console. If you aren't familiar with using the console, see Working with the AWS Management Console for an overview.

**To create an IAM user for yourself and add the user to an Administrators group**

1. Use your AWS account email address and password to sign in as the *AWS account root user* to the IAM console at https://console.aws.amazon.com/iam/. **Note**
   We strongly recommend that you adhere to the best practice of using the **Administrator** IAM user below and securely lock away the root user credentials. Sign in as the root user only to perform a few account and service management tasks.

2. In the navigation pane of the console, choose **Users**, and then choose **Add user**.

3. For **User name**, type **Administrator**.

4. Select the check box next to **AWS Management Console access**, select **Custom password**, and then type the new user's password in the text box. You can optionally select **Require password reset** to force the user to create a new password the next time the user signs in.

5. Choose **Next: Permissions**.

6. On the **Set permissions for user** page, choose **Add user to group**.

7. Choose **Create group**.

8. In the **Create group** dialog box, type **Administrators**.

9. For **Filter**, choose **Job function**.

10. In the policy list, select the check box for **AdministratorAccess**. Then choose **Create group**.

11. Back in the list of groups, select the check box for your new group. Choose **Refresh** if necessary to see the group in the list.

12. Choose **Next: Review** to see the list of group memberships to be added to the new user. When you are ready to proceed, choose **Create user**.

You can use this same process to create more groups and users, and to give your users access to your AWS account resources. To learn about using policies to restrict users' permissions to specific AWS resources, go to Access Management and Example Policies.

To sign in as this new IAM user, first sign out of the AWS console. Then use the following URL, where *your_aws_account_id* is your AWS account number without the hyphens. For example, if your AWS account number is 1234-5678-9012, your AWS account ID is 123456789012:

```
1 https://your_aws_account_id.signin.aws.amazon.com/console/
```

Enter the IAM user name and password that you just created. When you're signed in, the navigation bar displays *"your_user_name @ your_aws_account_id"*.

If you don't want the URL for your sign-in page to contain your AWS account ID, you can create an account alias. From the IAM dashboard, choose **Customize** and enter an alias, such as your company name. To sign in after you create an account alias, use the following URL:

```
1 https://your_account_alias.signin.aws.amazon.com/console/
```

To verify the sign-in link for IAM users for your account, open the IAM console and check under the **IAM users sign-in link** on the dashboard.

After you complete these steps, you can stop here and go to Getting Started with AWS WAF to continue getting started with AWS WAF using the console. If you want to access AWS WAF programmatically using the AWS WAF API, continue on to the next step, Step 3: Download Tools.

## Step 3: Download Tools

The AWS Management Console includes a console for AWS WAF, but if you want to access AWS WAF programmatically, the following documentation and tools will help you:

- If you want to call the AWS WAF API without having to handle low-level details like assembling raw HTTP requests, you can use an AWS SDK. The AWS SDKs provide functions and data types that encapsulate the functionality of AWS WAF and other AWS services. To download an AWS SDK, see the applicable page, which also includes prerequisites and installation instructions:

  - Java
  - JavaScript
  - .NET
  - Node.js
  - PHP
  - Python
  - Ruby

  For a complete list of AWS SDKs, see Tools for Amazon Web Services.

- If you're using a programming language for which AWS doesn't provide an SDK, the AWS WAF API Reference documents the operations that AWS WAF supports.

- The AWS Command Line Interface (AWS CLI) supports AWS WAF. The AWS CLI lets you control multiple AWS services from the command line and automate them through scripts. For more information, see AWS Command Line Interface.

- AWS Tools for Windows PowerShell supports AWS WAF. For more information, see AWS Tools for PowerShell Cmdlet Reference.

# AWS WAF

AWS WAF is a web application firewall that lets you monitor the HTTP and HTTPS requests that are forwarded to Amazon CloudFront or an Application Load Balancer. AWS WAF also lets you control access to your content. Based on conditions that you specify, such as the IP addresses that requests originate from or the values of query strings, CloudFront or an Application Load Balancer responds to requests either with the requested content or with an HTTP 403 status code (Forbidden). You also can configure CloudFront to return a custom error page when a request is blocked.

**Topics**

- How AWS WAF Works
- AWS WAF Pricing
- Getting Started with AWS WAF
- Tutorials
- Creating and Configuring a Web Access Control List (Web ACL)
- Listing IP addresses blocked by rate-based rules
- How AWS WAF Works with Amazon CloudFront Features
- Authentication and Access Control for AWS WAF
- AWS WAF Limits

# How AWS WAF Works

You use AWS WAF to control how Amazon CloudFront or an Application Load Balancer responds to web requests. You start by creating conditions, rules, and web access control lists (web ACLs). You define your conditions, combine your conditions into rules, and combine the rules into a web ACL.

**Conditions**

Conditions define the basic characteristics that you want AWS WAF to watch for in web requests:

- Scripts that are likely to be malicious. Attackers embed scripts that can exploit vulnerabilities in web applications. This is known as *cross-site scripting*.
- IP addresses or address ranges that requests originate from.
- Country or geographical location that requests originate from.
- Length of specified parts of the request, such as the query string.
- SQL code that is likely to be malicious. Attackers try to extract data from your database by embedding malicious SQL code in a web request. This is known as *SQL injection*.
- Strings that appear in the request, for example, values that appear in the `User-Agent` header or text strings that appear in the query string. You can also use regular expressions (regex) to specify these strings. Some conditions take multiple values. For example, you can specify up to 10,000 IP addresses or IP address ranges in an IP condition.

**Rules**

You combine conditions into rules to precisely target the requests that you want to allow, block, or count. AWS WAF provides two types of rules:

Regular rule

Regular rules use only conditions to target specific requests. For example, based on recent requests that you've seen from an attacker, you might create a rule that includes the following conditions:

- The requests come from 192.0.2.44.
- They contain the value `BadBot` in the `User-Agent` header.
- They appear to include SQL-like code in the query string. When a rule includes multiple conditions, as in this example, AWS WAF looks for requests that match all conditions—that is, it `AND`s the conditions together.

Rate-based rule

Rate-based rules are similar to regular rules, with one addition: a rate limit. Rate-based rules count the requests that arrive from a specified IP address every five minutes. The rule can trigger an action if the number of requests exceed the rate limit.

You can combine conditions with the rate limit. In this case, if the requests match all of the conditions and the number of requests exceed the rate limit in any five-minute period, the rule will trigger the action designated in the web ACL.

For example, based on recent requests that you've seen from an attacker, you might create a rate-based rule that includes the following conditions:

- The requests come from 192.0.2.44.
- They contain the value `BadBot` in the `User-Agent` header. In this rate-based rule, you also define a rate limit. In this example, let's say that you create a rate limit of 15,000. Requests that meet both of the preceding conditions and exceed 15,000 requests per five minutes trigger the rule's action (block or count), which is defined in the web ACL.

  Requests that do not meet both conditions will not be counted towards the rate limit and would not be blocked by this rule.

  As a second example, suppose that you want to limit requests to a particular page on your website. To do this, you could add the following string match condition to a rate-based rule:

- The **Part of the request to filter on** is URI.
- The **Match Type** is `Starts with`.
- A **Value to match** is `login`. Further, you specify a `RateLimit` of 15,000.

  By adding this rate-based rule to a web ACL, you could limit requests to your login page without affecting the rest of your site. You should add at least one condition to a regular rule. A regular rule with no conditions will not match any requests and therefore the rule's action (allow, count, block) will never be triggered.

However, conditions are optional for rate-based rules. If you don't add any conditions to a rate-based rule, AWS WAF assumes that *all* requests match the rule and therefore will be counted against the rate limit when arriving from the same IP address. Requests from the same IP address that exceed the rate limit will trigger the rule's action (count or block).

## Web ACLs

After you combine your conditions into rules, you combine the rules into a web ACL. This is where you define an action for each rule—allow, block, or count—and a default action:

## An action for each rule

When a web request matches all the conditions in a rule, AWS WAF can either block the request or allow the request to be forwarded to CloudFront or an Application Load Balancer. You specify the action that you want AWS WAF to perform for each rule.

AWS WAF compares a request with the rules in a web ACL in the order in which you listed the rules. AWS WAF then takes the action that is associated with the first rule that the request matches. For example, if a web request matches one rule that allows requests and another rule that blocks requests, AWS WAF will either allow or block the request depending on which rule is listed first.

If you want to test a new rule before you start using it, you also can configure AWS WAF to count the requests that meet all the conditions in the rule. As with rules that allow or block requests, a rule that counts requests is affected by its position in the list of rules in the web ACL. For example, if a web request matches a rule that allows requests and another rule that counts requests, and if the rule that allows requests is listed first, the request isn't counted.

## A default action

The default action determines whether AWS WAF allows or blocks a request that doesn't match all the conditions in any of the rules in the web ACL. For example, suppose you create a web ACL and add only the rule that you defined before:

- The requests come from 192.0.2.44.
- They contain the value `BadBot` in the `User-Agent` header.
- They appear to include malicious SQL code in the query string. If a request doesn't meet all three conditions in the rule and if the default action is `ALLOW`, AWS WAF forwards the request to CloudFront or an Application Load Balancer, and the service responds with the requested object.

  If you add two or more rules to a web ACL, AWS WAF performs the default action only if a request doesn't satisfy all the conditions in any of the rules. For example, suppose you add a second rule that contains one condition:
- Requests that contain the value `BIGBadBot` in the `User-Agent` header. AWS WAF performs the default action only when a request doesn't meet all three conditions in the first rule and doesn't meet the one condition in the second rule. On rare occasions, AWS WAF might encounter an internal error that delays the response to CloudFront or an Application Load Balancer about whether to allow or block a request. On those occasions, CloudFront or an Application Load Balancer typically will serve the content.

  The following illustration shows how AWS WAF checks the rules and performs the actions based on those rules.

**Web ACL**

Combines rules with an OR
- Checks rules in order listed
- Specifies action if rule is met
- Specifies default action if no rule is met

**Rate-based rule**
(combines conditions with an AND
and adds a rate limit)

**Condition**
Example: Cross-site scripting threat

AND

**Condition**
Example: Specific IP addresses

AND

**Rate limit: 15,000**

OR

**Rule**
(combines conditions with an AND)

**Condition**
Example: SQL injection threat

AND

**Condition**
Example: Specific string in header

If rule is met: do this action (Example: block)     If rule is met: do this action (Example: count)

If no rules match, perform default action (Example: allow)

# AWS WAF Pricing

With AWS WAF, you pay only for the web ACLs and rules that you create, and for the number of HTTP requests that AWS WAF inspects. For more information, see AWS WAF Pricing.

# Getting Started with AWS WAF

This tutorial shows how to use AWS WAF to perform the following tasks:

- Set up AWS WAF.
- Create a web access control list (web ACL) using the AWS WAF console, and specify the conditions that you want to use to filter web requests. For example, you can specify the IP addresses that the requests originate from and values in the request that are used only by attackers.
- Add the conditions to a rule. Rules let you target the web requests that you want to block or allow. A web request must match all the conditions in a rule before AWS WAF blocks or allows requests based on the conditions that you specify.
- Add the rules to your web ACL. This is where you specify whether you want to block web requests or allow them based on the conditions that you add to each rule.
- Specify a default action, either block or allow. This is the action that AWS WAF takes when a web request doesn't match any of your rules.
- Choose the Amazon CloudFront distribution that you want AWS WAF to inspect web requests for. This tutorial covers the steps only for CloudFront, but the process for an Application Load Balancer essentially is the same. AWS WAF for CloudFront is available for all regions. AWS WAF for use with an Application Load Balancer is available in the regions listed at AWS Regions and Endpoints.

**Note**
AWS typically bills you less than US $0.25 per day for the resources that you create during this tutorial. When you're finished with the tutorial, we recommend that you delete the resources to prevent incurring unnecessary charges.

**Topics**

- Step 1: Set Up AWS WAF
- Step 2: Create a Web ACL
- Step 3: Create an IP Match Condition
- Step 4: Create a Geo Match Condition
- Step 5: Create a String Match Condition
- Step 5A: Create a Regex Condition (Optional)
- Step 6: Create a SQL Injection Match Condition
- Step 7: (Optional) Create Additional Conditions
- Step 8: Create a Rule and Add Conditions
- Step 8: Add the Rule to a Web ACL
- Step 9: Clean Up Your Resources

## Step 1: Set Up AWS WAF

If you already signed up for an AWS account and created an IAM user as described in Setting Up, go to Step 2: Create a Web ACL.

If not, go to Setting Up and perform at least the first two steps. (You can skip downloading tools for now because this Getting Started topic focuses on using the AWS WAF console.)

## Step 2: Create a Web ACL

The AWS WAF console guides you through the process of configuring AWS WAF to block or allow web requests based on conditions that you specify, such as the IP addresses that the requests originate from or values in the requests. In this step, you create a web ACL.

**To create a web ACL**

1. Sign in to the AWS Management Console and open the AWS WAF console at https://console.aws.amazon.com/waf/.

2. If this is your first time using AWS WAF, choose **Go to AWS WAF**, and then choose **Configure web ACL**.

   If you've used AWS WAF before, choose **Web ACLs** in the navigation pane, and then choose **Create web ACL**.

3. On the **Name web ACL** page, for **Web ACL name**, type a name. **Note**
   You can't change the name after you create the web ACL.

4. For **CloudWatch metric name**, type a name. The name can contain only alphanumeric characters (A-Z, a-z, 0-9). It can't contain whitespace. **Note**
   You can't change the name after you create the web ACL.

5. For **Region**, choose a region. If you will associate this web ACL with a CloudFront distribution, choose **Global (CloudFront)**.

6. For **AWS resource to associate**, choose the resource that you want to associate with your web ACL, and then choose **Next**.

## Step 3: Create an IP Match Condition

An IP match condition specifies the IP addresses or IP address ranges that requests originate from. In this step, you create an IP match condition. In a later step, you specify whether you want to allow requests or block requests that originate from the specified IP addresses.

**Note**
For more information about IP match conditions, see Working with IP Match Conditions.

**To create an IP match condition**

1. On the **Create conditions** page, for **IP match conditions**, choose **Create condition**.

2. In the **Create IP match condition** dialog box, for **Name**, type a name. The name can contain only alphanumeric characters (A-Z, a-z, 0-9) or the following special characters: _-!"#'+*},./ .

3. For **Address**, type **192.0.2.0/24**. This IP address range, specified in CIDR notation, includes the IP addresses from 192.0.2.0 to 192.0.2.255. (The 192.0.2.0/24 IP address range is reserved for examples, so no web requests will originate from these IP addresses.)

   AWS WAF supports IPv4 address ranges: /8 and any range between /16 through /32. AWS WAF supports IPv6 address ranges: /16, /24, /32, /48, /56, /64, and /128. (To specify a single IP address, such as 192.0.2.44, type **192.0.2.44/32**.) Other ranges aren't supported.

   For more information about CIDR notation, see the Wikipedia article Classless Inter-Domain Routing.

4. Choose **Create**.

## Step 4: Create a Geo Match Condition

A geo match condition specifies the country or countries that requests originate from. In this step, you create a geo match condition. In a later step, you specify whether you want to allow requests or block requests that originate from the specified countries.

**Note**
For more information about geo match conditions, see Working with Geographic Match Conditions.

**To create a geo match condition**

1. On the **Create conditions** page, for **Geo match conditions**, choose **Create condition**.

2. In the **Create geo match condition** dialog box, for **Name**, type a name. The name can contain only alphanumeric characters (A-Z, a-z, 0-9) or the following special characters: _-!"#'+*},./ .

3. Choose a **Location type** and a country. **Location type** is currently limited to **Country**.

4. Choose **Add location**.

5. Choose **Create**.

## Step 5: Create a String Match Condition

A string match condition identifies the strings that you want AWS WAF to search for in a request, such as a specified value in a header or in a query string. Usually, a string consists of printable ASCII characters, but you can specify any character from hexadecimal 0x00 to 0xFF (decimal 0 to 255). In this step, you create a string match condition. In a later step, you specify whether you want to allow or block requests that contain the specified strings.

**Note**

For more information about string match conditions, see Working with String Match Conditions.

**To create a string match condition**

1. On the **Create conditions** page, for **String match conditions**, choose **Create condition**.

2. In the **Create string match condition** dialog box, type the following values:
   **Name**
   Type a name. The name can contain only alphanumeric characters (A-Z, a-z, 0-9) or the following special characters: _-!"#\+\*\},\./ \. **Type** Choose **String match**\. **Part of the request to filter on** Choose the part of the web request that you want AWS WAF to inspect for a specified string\. For this example, choose **Header**\. If you choose **Body** for the value of **Part of the request to filter on**, AWS WAF inspects only the first 8192 bytes \(8 KB\)because CloudFront forwards only the first 8192 bytes for inspection\. To allow or block requests for which the body is longer than 8192 bytes, you can create a size constraint condition\. \(AWS WAF gets the length of the body from the request headers\.\)For more information, see [Working with Size Constraint Conditions](web-acl-size-conditions.md)\. **Header \(Required if "Part of the request to filter on" is "Header"\)** Because you chose **Header** for **Part of the request to filter on**, you must specify which header you want AWS WAF to inspect\. Type **User\-Agent**\. \(This value is not case sensitive\.\)**Match type** Choose where the specified string must appear in the **User\-Agent** header, for example, at the beginning, at the end, or anywhere in the string\. For this example, choose **Exactly matches**, which indicates that AWS WAF inspects web requests for a header value that is identical to the value that you specify\. **Transformation** In an effort to bypass AWS WAF, attackers use unusual formatting in web requests, for example, by adding whitespace or by URL\-encoding some or all of the request\. Transformations convert the web request to a more standard format by removing whitespace, by URL\-decoding the request, or by performing other operations that eliminate much of the unusual formatting that attackers commonly use\. You can only specify a single type of text transformation\. For this example, choose **None**\. **Value is base64 encoded** When the value that you type in **Value to match** is already base64\-encoded, select this check box\. For this example, don't select the check box\. **Value to match** Specify the value that you want AWS WAF to search for in the part of web requests that you indicated in **Part of the request to filter on**\. For this example, type **BadBot**\. AWS WAF will inspect theUser-Agent' header in web requests for the value **BadBot**.
   The maximum length of **Value to match** is 50 characters. If you want to specify a base64-encoded value, the limit is 50 characters before encoding.

3. If you want AWS WAF to inspect web requests for multiple values, such as a `User-Agent` header that contains `BadBot` and a query string that contains `BadParameter`, you have two choices:

- If you want to allow or block web requests only when they contain both values (`AND`), you create one string match condition for each value.
- If you want to allow or block web requests when they contain either value or both (`OR`), you add both values to the same string match condition.

For this example, choose **Create**.

## Step 5A: Create a Regex Condition (Optional)

A regular expression condition is a type of string match condition and similar in that it identifies the strings that you want AWS WAF to search for in a request, such as a specified value in a header or in a query string. The primary difference is that you use a regular expression (regex) to specify the string pattern that you want AWS WAF to search for. In this step, you create a regex match condition. In a later step, you specify whether you want to allow or block requests that contain the specified strings.

**Note**
For more information about regex match conditions, see Working with Regex Match Conditions.

**To create a regex match condition**

1. On the **Create conditions** page, for **String match conditions**, choose **Create condition**.

2. In the **Create string match condition** dialog box, type the following values:
**Name**
Type a name. The name can contain only alphanumeric characters (A-Z, a-z, 0-9) or the following special characters:   \_-!"#\+\*\},\./ \. **Type** Choose **Regex match**\. **Part of the request to filter on** Choose the part of the web request that you want AWS WAF to inspect for a specified string\. For this example, choose **Body**\. If you choose **Body** for the value of **Part of the request to filter on**, AWS WAF inspects only the first 8192 bytes \(8 KB\)because CloudFront forwards only the first 8192 bytes for inspection\. To allow or block requests for which the body is longer than 8192 bytes, you can create a size constraint condition\. \(AWS WAF gets the length of the body from the request headers\.\)For more information, see [Working with Size Constraint Conditions]\(web-acl -size-conditions.md\)\. **Transformation** In an effort to bypass AWS WAF, attackers use unusual formatting in web requests, for example, by adding whitespace or by URL\- encoding some or all of the request\. Transformations convert the web request to a more standard format by removing whitespace, by URL\-decoding the request, or by performing other operations that eliminate much of the unusual formatting that attackers commonly use\. You can only specify a single type of text transformation\. For this example, choose **None**\. **Regex patterns to match to request** Choose **Create regex pattern set**\. **New pattern set name** Type a name and then specify the regex pattern that you want AWS WAF to search for\. Next, type the regular expression **I\[a@\]mAB\[a@\] dRequest**\. AWS WAF will inspect theUser-Agent' header in web requests for the values:

- IamABadRequest
- IamAB@dRequest
- I@mABadRequest
- I@mAB@dRequest

3. Choose **Create pattern set and add filter**.

4. Choose **Create**.

## Step 6: Create a SQL Injection Match Condition

A SQL injection match condition identifies the part of web requests, such as a header or a query string, that you want AWS WAF to inspect for malicious SQL code. Attackers use SQL queries to extract data from your database. In this step, you create a SQL injection match condition. In a later step, you specify whether you want to allow requests or block requests that appear to contain malicious SQL code.

**Note**
For more information about string match conditions, see Working with SQL Injection Match Conditions.

**To create a SQL injection match condition**

1. On the **Create conditions** page, for **SQL injection match conditions**, choose **Create condition**.

2. In the **Create SQL injection match condition** dialog box, type the following values:
   **Name**
   Type a name.
   **Part of the request to filter on**
   Choose the part of web requests that you want AWS WAF to inspect for malicious SQL code.
   For this example, choose **Query string**.
   If you choose **Body** for the value of **Part of the request to filter on**, AWS WAF inspects only the first 8192 bytes (8 KB) because CloudFront forwards only the first 8192 bytes for inspection. To allow or block requests for which the body is longer than 8192 bytes, you can create a size constraint condition. (AWS WAF gets the length of the body from the request headers.) For more information, see Working with Size Constraint Conditions.
   **Transformation**
   For this example, choose **URL decode**.
   Attackers use unusual formatting, such as URL encoding, in an effort to bypass AWS WAF. The **URL decode** option eliminates some of that formatting in the web request before AWS WAF inspects the request.
   You can only specify a single type of text transformation.

3. Choose **Create**.

4. Choose **Next**.

## Step 7: (Optional) Create Additional Conditions

AWS WAF includes other conditions, including the following:

- **Size constraint conditions** – Identifies the part of web requests, such as a header or a query string, that you want AWS WAF to check for length. For more information, see Working with Size Constraint Conditions.
- **Cross-site scripting match conditions** – Identifies the part of web requests, such as a header or a query string, that you want AWS WAF to inspect for malicious scripts. For more information, see Working with Cross-site Scripting Match Conditions.

You can optionally create these conditions now, or you can skip to Step 8: Create a Rule and Add Conditions.

## Step 8: Create a Rule and Add Conditions

You create a rule to specify the conditions that you want AWS WAF to search for in web requests. If you add more than one condition to a rule, a web request must match all the conditions in the rule for AWS WAF to allow or block requests based on that rule.

**Note**
For more information about rules, see Working with Rules.

**To create a rule and add conditions**

1. On the **Create rules** page, choose **Create rule**.

2. In the **Create rule** dialog box, type the following values:
   **Name**
   Type a name.
   **CloudWatch metric name**
   Type a name for the CloudWatch metric that AWS WAF will create and will associate with the rule. The name can contain only alphanumeric characters (A-Z, a-z, 0-9). It can't contain whitespace.
   **Rule type**
   Choose either `Regular rule` or `Rate based rule`. Rate based rules are identical to regular rules but also take into account how many requests arrive from the identified IP address every five minutes. For more information on these rule types, see How AWS WAF Works. For this example, choose `Regular rule`.
   **Rate limit**
   If you are creating a rate-based rule, enter the maximum number of requests from a single IP address allowed in a five-minute period.

3. For the first condition that you want to add to the rule, specify the following settings:

   - Choose whether you want AWS WAF to allow or block requests based on whether a web request does or does not match the settings in the condition.

     For this example, choose **does**.

   - Choose the type of condition that you want to add to the rule: an IP match set condition, a string match set condition, or a SQL injection match set condition.

     For this example, choose **originate from IP addresses in**.

   - Choose the condition that you want to add to the rule.

     For this example, choose the IP match condition that you created in previous tasks.

4. Choose **Add condition**.

5. Add the geo match condition that you created earlier. Specify the following values:

   - **When a request does**
   - **originate from a geographic location in**
   - Choose your geo match condition.

6. Choose **Add another condition**.

7. Add the string match condition that you created earlier. Specify the following values:

   - **When a request does**
   - **match at least one of the filters in the string match condition**
   - Choose your string match condition.

8. Choose **Add condition**.

9. Add the SQL injection match condition that you created earlier. Specify the following values:

   - **When a request does**
   - **match at least one of the filters in the SQL injection match condition**
   - Choose your SQL injection match condition.

10. Choose **Add condition**.

11. Add the size constraint condition that you created earlier. Specify the following values:

    - **When a request does**
    - **match at least one of the filters in the size constraint condition**
    - Choose your size constraint condition.

12. If you created any other conditions, such as a regex condition, add those in a similar manner.

13. Choose **Create**.

14. For the **Default action**, choose **Allow all requests that don't match any rules**.

15. Choose **Review and create**.

## Step 8: Add the Rule to a Web ACL

When you add the rule to a web ACL, you specify the following settings:

- The action that you want AWS WAF to take on web requests that match all the conditions in the rule: allow, block, or count the requests.
- The default action for the web ACL. This is the action that you want AWS WAF to take on web requests that *do not* match all the conditions in the rule: allow or block the requests.

AWS WAF starts blocking CloudFront web requests that match all the following conditions (and any others you might have added):

- The value of the `User-Agent` header is `BadBot`
- (If you created and added the regex condition) The value of the `Body` is any of the four strings that matches the pattern `I[a@]mAB[a@]dRequest`
- The requests originate from IP addresses in the range 192.0.2.0-192.0.2.255
- The requests originate from country you selected in your geo match condition
- The requests appear to include malicious SQL code in the query string

AWS WAF allows CloudFront to respond to any requests that don't meet all three of these conditions.

## Step 9: Clean Up Your Resources

You've now successfully completed the tutorial. To prevent your account from accruing additional AWS WAF charges, you should clean up the AWS WAF objects that you created. Alternatively, you can change the configuration to match the web requests that you really want to allow, block, and count.

**Note**
AWS typically bills you less than US $0.25 per day for the resources that you create during this tutorial. When you're finished, we recommend that you delete the resources to prevent incurring unnecessary charges.

**To delete the objects that AWS WAF charges for**

1. Disassociate your web ACL from your CloudFront distribution:

    1. Sign in to the AWS Management Console and open the AWS WAF console at https://console.aws.amazon.com/waf/.

    2. Choose the web ACL that you want to delete.

    3. In the right pane, on the **Rules** tab, go to the **AWS resources using this web ACL** section. For the CloudFront distribution that you associated the web ACL with, choose the **x** in the **Type** column.

2. Remove the conditions from your rule:

    1. In the navigation pane, choose **Rules**.

    2. Choose the rule that you created during the tutorial.

    3. Choose **Edit rule**.

    4. Choose the **x** at the right of each condition heading.

    5. Choose **Update**.

3. Remove the rule from your web ACL, and delete the web ACL:

    1. In the navigation pane, choose **Web ACLs**.

    2. Choose the web ACL that you created during the tutorial.

    3. On the **Rules** tab, choose **Edit web ACL**.

    4. Choose the **x** at the right of the rule heading.

    5. Choose **Actions**, and then choose **Delete web ACL**.

4. Delete your rule:

    1. In the navigation pane, choose **Rules**.

    2. Choose the rule that you created during the tutorial.

    3. Choose **Delete**.

    4. In the **Delete** dialog box, choose **Delete** again to confirm.

AWS WAF doesn't charge for conditions, but if you want to complete the cleanup, perform the following procedure to remove filters from conditions and delete the conditions.

**To delete filters and conditions**

1. Delete the IP address range in your IP match condition, and delete the IP match condition:

    1. In the navigation pane of the AWS WAF console, choose **IP addresses**.

    2. Choose the IP match condition that you created during the tutorial.

    3. Select the check box for the IP address range that you added.

    4. Choose **Delete IP address or range**.

    5. In the **IP match conditions** pane, choose **Delete**.

    6. In the **Delete** dialog box, choose **Delete** again to confirm.

2. Delete the filter in your SQL injection match condition, and delete the SQL injection match condition:

    1. In the navigation pane, choose **SQL injection**.

    2. Choose the SQL injection match condition that you created during the tutorial.

    3. Select the check box for the filter that you added.

    4. Choose **Delete filter**.

    5. In the **SQL injection match conditions** pane, choose **Delete**.

    6. In the **Delete** dialog box, choose **Delete** again to confirm.

3. Delete the filter in your string match condition, and delete the string match condition:

    1. In the navigation pane, choose **String and regex matching**.

    2. Choose the string match condition that you created during the tutorial.

    3. Select the check box for the filter that you added.

    4. Choose **Delete filter**.

    5. In the **String match conditions** pane, choose **Delete**.

    6. In the **Delete** dialog box, choose **Delete** again to confirm.

4. If you created one, delete the filter in your regex match condition, and delete the regex match condition:

    1. In the navigation pane, choose **String and regex matching**.

2. Choose the regex match condition that you created during the tutorial.

3. Select the check box for the filter that you added.

4. Choose **Delete filter**.

5. In the **Regex match conditions** pane, choose **Delete**.

6. In the **Delete** dialog box, choose **Delete** again to confirm.

5. Delete the filter in your size constraint condition, and delete the size constraint condition:

1. In the navigation pane, choose **Size constraints**.

2. Choose the size constraint condition that you created during the tutorial.

3. Select the check box for the filter that you added.

4. Choose **Delete filter**.

5. In the **Size constraint conditions** pane, choose **Delete**.

6. In the **Delete** dialog box, choose **Delete** again to confirm.

# Tutorials

This section contains a link to a preconfigured template as well as three tutorials that present complete solutions for common tasks that you can perform in AWS WAF. The tutorials show how to combine several AWS services to automatically configure AWS WAF in response to your CloudFront traffic. Their purpose is to provide general guidance. They are not intended for direct use in your production environment without careful review and adaptation to the unique aspects of your business environment.

**AWS WAF Preconfigured Protections**

You can use our preconfigured template to get started quickly with AWS WAF. The template includes a set of AWS WAF rules that are designed to block common web-based attacks. You can customize the template to fit your business needs.

The rules in the template help protect against bad bots, SQL injection, cross-site scripting (XSS), HTTP floods, and other known attacks. After you deploy the template, AWS WAF begins to block the web requests to your CloudFront distributions or Application Load Balancers that match the preconfigured rules in your web access control (web ACL) list. You can use this automated solution in addition to other web ACLs that you configure. For more information, see AWS WAF Security Automations.

**Tutorials**

- Tutorial: Quickly Setting Up AWS WAF Protection Against Common Attacks
- Tutorial: Blocking IP Addresses That Submit Bad Requests
- Tutorial: Implementing a DDoS-resistant Website Using AWS Services

# Tutorial: Quickly Setting Up AWS WAF Protection Against Common Attacks

This tutorial shows you how to use AWS CloudFormation to quickly configure AWS WAF to protect against the following common attacks:

- **Cross-site scripting attacks** – Attackers sometimes insert scripts into web requests in an effort to exploit vulnerabilities in web applications. Cross-site scripting match conditions identify the parts of web requests, such as the URI or the query string, that you want AWS WAF to inspect for possible malicious scripts.
- **SQL injection attacks** – Attackers sometimes insert malicious SQL code into web requests in an effort to extract data from your database. SQL injection match conditions identify the part of web requests that you want AWS WAF to inspect for possible malicious SQL code.
- **Attacks from known bad IP addresses** – You can use IP match conditions to allow, block, or count web requests based on the IP addresses that the requests originate from. An IP match condition lists up to 1,000 IP addresses or IP address ranges that you specify.

**Note**

This tutorial assumes that you have a CloudFront distribution that you use to deliver content for your web application. If you don't have a CloudFront distribution, see Creating or Updating a Web Distribution Using the CloudFront Console in the *Amazon CloudFront Developer Guide*.

**Topics**

- Solution Overview
- Step 1: Create an AWS CloudFormation Stack That Sets Up AWS WAF Protection Against Common Attacks
- Step 2: Associate a Web ACL with a CloudFront Distribution
- Step 3: (Optional) Add IP Addresses to the IP Match Condition
- Step 4: (Optional) Update the Web ACL to Block Large Bodies
- Step 5: (Optional) Delete Your AWS CloudFormation Stack
- Related Resources

## Solution Overview

AWS CloudFormation uses a template to set up the following AWS WAF conditions, rules, and a web ACL.

### Conditions

AWS CloudFormation creates the following conditions.

**IP Match Condition**

Filters requests that come from known bad IP addresses. This lets you easily add IPs to a list to block access to your website. You might want to do this if you're receiving a lot of bad requests from one or more IP addresses. If you want to allow, block, or count requests based on the IP addresses that the requests come from, see Step 3: (Optional) Add IP Addresses to the IP Match Condition later in this tutorial.

The name of the condition is *prefix***ManualBlockSet** where *prefix* is the name that you specify for the web ACL when you create the AWS CloudFormation stack.

**Size Constraint Condition**

Filters requests for which the body is longer than 8,192 bytes. AWS WAF evaluates only the first 8,192 bytes of the request part that you specify in a filter. If valid request bodies never exceed 8,192 bytes, you can use a size constraint condition to catch malicious requests that might otherwise slip through.

For this tutorial, AWS CloudFormation configures AWS WAF only to count, not block, requests that have a body longer than 8,192 bytes. If the body in your requests never exceeds that length, you can change the configuration to block requests that have longer bodies. For information about how to view the count of requests that exceed 8,192 bytes and how to change the web ACL to block requests that contain bodies larger than 8,192 bytes, see Step 4: (Optional) Update the Web ACL to Block Large Bodies.

The name of the condition is *prefix***LargeBodyMatch** where *prefix* is the name that you specify for the web ACL when you create the AWS CloudFormation stack.

## SQL Injection Condition

Filters requests that contain possible malicious SQL code. The condition includes filters that evaluate the following parts of requests:

- Query string (URL decode transformation)
- URI (URL decode transformation)
- Body (URL decode transformation)
- Body (HTML decode transformation) The name of the condition is *prefix***SqliMatch** where *prefix* is the name that you specify for the web ACL when you create the AWS CloudFormation stack.

## Cross-site Scripting Condition

Filters requests that contain possible malicious scripts. The condition includes filters that evaluate the following parts of requests:

- Query string (URL decode transformation)
- URI (URL decode transformation)
- Body (URL decode transformation)
- Body (HTML decode transformation) The name of the condition is *prefix***XssMatch** where *prefix* is the name that you specify for the web ACL when you create the AWS CloudFormation stack.

## Rules

When you create the AWS CloudFormation stack, AWS CloudFormation creates the following rules and adds the corresponding condition to each rule:

### *prefix*ManualIPBlockRule
AWS CloudFormation adds the *prefix***ManualBlockSet** condition to this rule.

### *prefix*SizeMatchRule
AWS CloudFormation adds the *prefix***LargeBodyMatch** condition to this rule.

### *prefix*SqliRule
AWS CloudFormation adds the *prefix***SqliMatch** condition to this rule.

### *prefix*XssRule
AWS CloudFormation adds the *prefix***XssMatch** condition to this rule.

## Web ACL

AWS CloudFormation creates a web ACL that has the name that you specify when you create the AWS CloudFormation stack. The web ACL contains the following rules with the specified settings:

### *prefix*ManualIPBlockRule
By default, the condition in this rule doesn't contain any IP addresses. If you want to allow, block, or count requests based on the IP addresses that the requests come from, see Step 3: (Optional) Add IP Addresses to the IP Match Condition later in this tutorial.

### *prefix*SizeMatchRule
By default, AWS WAF counts requests for which the body is longer than 8,192 bytes.

### *prefix*SqliRule
AWS WAF blocks requests based on the settings in this rule.

*prefix*XssRule
AWS WAF blocks requests based on the settings in this rule.

## Requirements

This tutorial assumes that you have a CloudFront distribution that you use to deliver content for your web application. If you don't have a CloudFront distribution, see Creating or Updating a Web Distribution Using the CloudFront Console in the *Amazon CloudFront Developer Guide*. This tutorial also uses AWS CloudFormation to simplify the provisioning process. For more information, see the AWS CloudFormation User Guide.

## Estimated Time

The estimated time to complete this tutorial is 15 minutes if you already have a CloudFront distribution, or 30 minutes if you need to create a CloudFront distribution.

## Costs

There is a cost associated with the resources that you create during this tutorial. You can delete the resources after you finish the tutorial to stop incurring charges. For more information, see AWS WAF Pricing and Amazon CloudFront Pricing.

## Step 1: Create an AWS CloudFormation Stack That Sets Up AWS WAF Protection Against Common Attacks

In the following procedure, you use an AWS CloudFormation template to create a stack that sets up AWS WAF protection against common attacks.

**Important**
You begin to incur charges for the different services when you create the AWS CloudFormation stack that deploys this solution. Charges continue to accrue until you delete the AWS CloudFormation stack. For more information, see Step 5: (Optional) Delete Your AWS CloudFormation Stack.

**To create an AWS CloudFormation stack for blocking IP addresses that submit bad requests**

1. To start the process that creates an AWS CloudFormation stack, choose the link for the region in which you want to create AWS resources:

   - Create a stack in US East (N. Virginia)
   - Create a stack in US West (Oregon)
   - Create a stack in EU (Ireland)
   - Create a stack in Asia Pacific (Tokyo)

2. If you are not already signed in to the AWS Management Console, sign in when prompted.

3. On the **Select Template** page, choose **Specify an Amazon S3 template URL**. For the template URL, type **https://s3/.amazonaws/.com/cloudformation/-examples/community/common/-attacks/.json**/.

4. Choose **Next**.

5. On the **Specify Details** page, specify the following values:
   **Stack Name**
   You can use the default name (**CommonAttackProtection**), or you can change the name. The stack name must not contain spaces and must be unique within your AWS account.
   **Name**
   Specify a name for the web ACL that AWS CloudFormation will create. The name that you specify is also

used as a prefix for the conditions and rules that AWS CloudFormation will create, so you can easily find all the related objects.

6. Choose **Next**.

7. (Optional) On the **Options** page, enter tags and advanced settings or leave the boxes blank.

8. Choose **Next**.

9. On the **Review** page, review the configuration, and then choose **Create**.

After you choose **Create**, AWS CloudFormation creates the AWS WAF resources that are identified in Solution Overview.

## Step 2: Associate a Web ACL with a CloudFront Distribution

After AWS CloudFormation creates the stack, you must associate your CloudFront distribution to activate AWS WAF.

**Note**
You can associate a web ACL with as many distributions as you want, but you can associate only one web ACL with a given distribution.

**To associate a web ACL with a CloudFront distribution**

1. Sign in to the AWS Management Console and open the AWS WAF console at https://console.aws.amazon.com/waf/.

2. In the navigation pane, choose **Web ACLs**.

3. Choose the web ACL that you want to associate with a CloudFront distribution.

4. On the **Rules** tab, under **AWS resources using this web ACL**, choose **Add association**.

5. When prompted, use the **Resource** list to choose the distribution that you want to associate this web ACL with.

6. Choose **Add**.

7. To associate this web ACL with additional CloudFront distributions, repeat steps 4 through 6.

## Step 3: (Optional) Add IP Addresses to the IP Match Condition

When you created the AWS CloudFormation stack, AWS CloudFormation created an IP match condition for you, added it to a rule, added the rule to a web ACL, and configured the web ACL to block requests based on IP addresses. The IP match condition doesn't include any IP addresses, though. If you want to block requests based on IP addresses, perform the following procedure.

**To edit AWS CloudFormation parameter values**

1. Open the AWS WAF console at https://console.aws.amazon.com/waf/.

2. In the navigation pane, choose **IP addresses**.

3. In the **IP match conditions** pane, choose the IP match condition that you want to edit.

4. To add an IP address range:

   1. In the right pane, choose **Add IP address or range**.

   2. Type an IP address or range by using CIDR notation. Here are two examples:

      - To specify the IP address 192.0.2.44, type **192.0.2.44/32**.
      - To specify the range of IP addresses from 192.0.2.0 to 192.0.2.255, type **192.0.2.0/24**.

AWS WAF supports IPv4 address ranges: /8 and any range between /16 through /32. AWS WAF supports IPv6 address ranges: /16, /24, /32, /48, /56, /64, and /128. For more information about CIDR notation, see the Wikipedia entry Classless Inter-Domain Routing. **Note**
AWS WAF supports both IPv4 and IPv6 IP addresses.

3. To add more IP addresses, choose **Add another IP address**, and then type the value.

4. Choose **Add**.

## Step 4: (Optional) Update the Web ACL to Block Large Bodies

When you created the AWS CloudFormation stack, AWS CloudFormation created a size constraint condition that filters requests that have request bodies longer than 8,192 bytes. It also added the condition to a rule, and added the rule to the web ACL. In this example, AWS CloudFormation configured the web ACL to count requests, not to block requests. This is useful when you want to confirm you are not blocking valid requests inadvertently.

If you want to block requests that are longer than 8,192 bytes, perform the following procedure.

**To change the action for a rule in a web ACL**

1. Open the AWS WAF console at https://console.aws.amazon.com/waf/.

2. In the navigation pane, choose **Web ACLs**.

3. Choose the web ACL that you want to edit.

4. In the right pane, choose the **Rules** tab.

5. Choose **Edit Web ACL**.

6. To change the action for the *prefix***LargeBodyMatchRule**, choose the preferred option. (*prefix* is the value that you specified for the name of the web ACL.)

7. Choose **Save changes**.

## Step 5: (Optional) Delete Your AWS CloudFormation Stack

If you want to stop protecting from common attacks as described in Solution Overview, delete the AWS CloudFormation stack that you created in Step 1: Create an AWS CloudFormation Stack That Sets Up AWS WAF Protection Against Common Attacks. This deletes the AWS WAF resources that AWS CloudFormation created and stops the AWS charges for those resources.

**To delete an AWS CloudFormation stack**

1. Sign in to the AWS Management Console and open the AWS CloudFormation console at https://console.aws.amazon.com/cloudformation.

2. Select the check box for the stack. The default name is **CommonAttackProtection**.

3. Choose **Delete Stack**.

4. Choose **Yes, Delete** to confirm.

5. To track the progress of the stack deletion, select the check box for the stack, and choose the **Events** tab in the bottom pane.

## Related Resources

For AWS WAF samples, including Lambda functions, AWS CloudFormation templates, and SDK usage examples, go to GitHub at https://github.com/awslabs/aws-waf-sample.

# Tutorial: Blocking IP Addresses That Submit Bad Requests

Using AWS Lambda, you can set a threshold of how many bad requests per minute your web application will tolerate from a given IP address. A bad request is one for which your CloudFront origin returns one of the following HTTP 40x status codes:

- 400, Bad Request
- 403, Forbidden
- 404, Not Found
- 405, Method Not Allowed

If users (based on IP addresses) exceed this error code threshold, Lambda automatically updates your AWS WAF rules to block IP addresses and specify for how long requests from those IP addresses should be blocked.

This tutorial shows you how to use an AWS CloudFormation template to specify the request threshold and time to block requests. The tutorial also uses CloudFront access logs (stored in Amazon S3) to count requests as they are served by CloudFront and by Amazon CloudWatch metrics.

### Topics

- Solution Overview
- Step 1: Create an AWS CloudFormation Stack for Blocking IP Addresses That Submit Bad Requests
- Step 2: Associate a Web ACL with a CloudFront Distribution
- Step 3: (Optional) Edit AWS CloudFormation Parameter Values
- Step 4: (Optional) Test Your Thresholds and IP Rules
- Step 5: (Optional) Delete Your AWS CloudFormation Stack
- Related Resources

## Solution Overview

The following illustration shows how you can use AWS WAF with AWS Lambda to block requests from specific IP addresses.

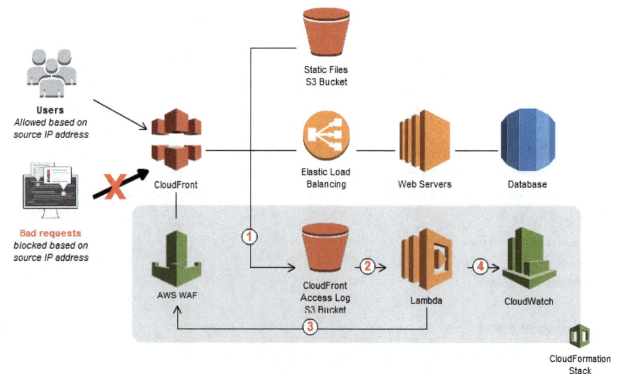

1. As CloudFront receives requests on behalf of your web application, it sends access logs to an Amazon S3 bucket that contains detailed information about the requests.

2. For every new access log stored in the Amazon S3 bucket, a Lambda function is triggered. The Lambda function parses the log files and looks for requests that resulted in error codes 400, 403, 404, and 405. The function then counts the number of bad requests and temporarily stores results in `current_outstanding_requesters.json` in the Amazon S3 bucket that you're using for access logs.

3. The Lambda function updates AWS WAF rules to block the IP addresses that are listed in `current_outstanding_requesters.json` for a period of time that you specify. After this blocking period has expired, AWS WAF allows those IP addresses to access your application again, but continues to monitor the requests from those IP addresses.

4. The Lambda function publishes execution metrics in CloudWatch, such as the number of requests analyzed and IP addresses blocked.

The AWS CloudFormation template creates a web access control list (web ACL) and two separate rules in AWS WAF that block and monitor requests from IP addresses, depending on the settings that you configure during the tutorial. The two rules are defined here:

- **Auto Block** – This rule adds IP addresses that exceed the request-per-minute limit. New requests from those IP addresses are blocked until Lambda removes the IP addresses from the block list after the specified expiration period. The default is four hours.
- **Manual Block** – This rule adds IP addresses manually to the auto-block list. The IP addresses are permanently blocked; they can access the web application only if you remove them from the block list. You can use this list to block known bad IP addresses or IP addresses that frequently are added to the auto-block rule.

**Requirements:** This tutorial assumes that you already have a CloudFront distribution that you use to deliver content for your web application. If you don't have a CloudFront distribution, see Creating or Updating a Web Distribution Using the CloudFront Console in the *Amazon CloudFront Developer Guide*. This tutorial also uses AWS CloudFormation to simplify the provisioning process. For more information, see the AWS CloudFormation User Guide.

**Estimated time:** 15 minutes if you already have a CloudFront distribution, or 30 minutes if you need to create a CloudFront distribution.

**Estimated cost:**

- **AWS WAF**
  - $5.00 per month per web ACL (the tutorial creates one web ACL)
  - $1.00 per month per rule (x2 for the two rules that AWS CloudFormation creates for this tutorial)
  - $0.60 per million requests
- **AWS Lambda** – Each new CloudFront access log represents a new request and triggers the Lambda function that is created by this tutorial. Lambda charges include the following:
  - **Requests** – The first million requests are free, and then Lambda charges $0.20 per million requests. CloudFront delivers access logs for a distribution up to several times an hour.
  - **Memory used per second** – $0.00001667 per GB of memory used per second.
- **Amazon S3** – Amazon S3 charges for storing CloudFront access logs. The size of the logs and, therefore, the charge for storage depends on the number of requests that CloudFront receives for your objects. For more information, see Amazon S3 Pricing.
- **CloudFront** – You don't incur any additional CloudFront charges for this solution. For more information, see Amazon CloudFront Pricing.

## Step 1: Create an AWS CloudFormation Stack for Blocking IP Addresses That Submit Bad Requests

In the following procedure, you use an AWS CloudFormation template to create a stack that launches the AWS resources required by Lambda, CloudFront, Amazon S3, AWS WAF, and CloudWatch.

**Important**

You begin to incur charges for the different services when you create the AWS CloudFormation stack that deploys this solution. Charges continue to accrue until you delete the AWS CloudFormation stack. For more information, see Step 5: (Optional) Delete Your AWS CloudFormation Stack.

**To create an AWS CloudFormation stack for blocking IP addresses that submit bad requests**

1. To start the process that creates an AWS CloudFormation stack, choose the link for the region in which you want to create AWS resources:

   - Create a stack in US East (N. Virginia)
   - Create a stack in US West (Oregon)
   - Create a stack in EU (Ireland)
   - Create a stack in Asia Pacific (Tokyo)

2. If you are not already signed in to the AWS Management Console, sign in when prompted.

3. On the **Select Template** page, the selected URL automatically appears under **Specify an Amazon S3 template URL**. Choose **Next**.

4. On the **Specify Details** page, specify the following values:
   **Stack Name**
   You can use the default name (**BadBehavingIP**), or you can change the name. The stack name must not contain spaces and must be unique within your AWS account.
   **Create CloudFront Access Log Bucket**
   Select **yes** to create a new Amazon S3 bucket for CloudFront access logs, or select **no** if you already have an Amazon S3 bucket for CloudFront access logs.
   **CloudFront Access Log Bucket Name**
   Type the name of the Amazon S3 bucket where you want CloudFront to put access logs. Leave this box empty if you selected **no** for **Create CloudFront Access Log Bucket**.
   **Request Threshold**
   Type the maximum number of requests that can be made from an IP address per minute without being blocked. The default is 400.
   **WAF Block Period**
   Specify how long (in minutes) an IP address should be blocked after crossing the threshold. The default is 240 minutes (four hours).

5. Choose **Next**.

6. (Optional) On the **Options** page, enter tags and advanced settings or leave the boxes blank.

7. Choose **Next**.

8. On the **Review** page, select the **I acknowledge** check box, and then choose **Create**.

   After you choose **Create**, AWS CloudFormation creates the AWS resources that are necessary to run the solution:

   - Lambda function
   - AWS WAF web ACL (named **Malicious Requesters**) with the necessary rules configured
   - CloudWatch custom metric
   - Amazon S3 bucket with the name that you specified in the **CloudFront Access Log Bucket Name** field in step 6, if you selected **yes** for **Create CloudFront Access Log Bucket**

## Step 2: Associate a Web ACL with a CloudFront Distribution

After AWS CloudFormation creates the stack, you must associate the CloudFront distribution to activate AWS WAF and update your Amazon S3 bucket to enable event notification.

**Note**
If you're already using AWS WAF to monitor CloudFront requests and if logging is already enabled for the distribution that you're monitoring, you can skip the first procedure.

**Note**
You can associate a web ACL with as many distributions as you want, but you can associate only one web ACL with a given distribution.

**To associate a web ACL with a CloudFront distribution**

1. Sign in to the AWS Management Console and open the AWS WAF console at https://console.aws.amazon.com/waf/.

2. In the navigation pane, choose **Web ACLs**.

3. Choose the web ACL that you want to associate with a CloudFront distribution.

4. On the **Rules** tab, under **AWS resources using this web ACL**, choose **Add association**.

5. When prompted, use the **Resource** list to choose the distribution that you want to associate this web ACL with.

6. Choose **Add**.

7. To associate this web ACL with additional CloudFront distributions, repeat steps 4 through 6.

If you already have an Amazon S3 bucket for CloudFront access logs (if you selected **no** for **Create CloudFront Access Log Bucket** in the preceding procedure), enable Amazon S3 event notification to trigger the Lambda function when a new log file is added to the bucket. For more information, see Enabling Event Notifications in the *Amazon Simple Storage Service Console User Guide*.

**Note**
If you chose to have AWS CloudFormation create the bucket for you, AWS CloudFormation also enabled event notifications for the bucket.

**To enable Amazon S3 event notification**

1. Open the Amazon S3 console at https://console.aws.amazon.com/s3/.

2. Choose the bucket that you want to use for CloudFront access logs.

3. Choose **Properties**, and expand **Events**.

4. Specify the following values:
   **Name**
   Type a name for the event, such as **LambdaNotificationsForWAFBadRequests**. The name cannot contain spaces.
   **Events**
   Select **ObjectCreated (All)**.
   **Prefix**
   Leave the field empty.
   **Suffix**
   Type **gz**.
   **Send To**
   Select **Lambda function**.
   **Lambda function**
   Choose **BadBehavingIP** or the name that you specified for your AWS CloudFormation stack.

5. Choose **Save**.

## Step 3: (Optional) Edit AWS CloudFormation Parameter Values

If you want to change the parameters after you create the AWS CloudFormation stack—for example, if you want to change the threshold value or how long IPs are blocked—you can update the AWS CloudFormation stack.

**To edit AWS CloudFormation parameter values**

1. Open the AWS CloudFormation console at https://console.aws.amazon.com/cloudformation.

2. In the list of stacks, choose the running stack that you want to update, which is **BadBehavingIP** if you accepted the default value when you created the stack.

3. Choose **Actions**, and then choose **Update Stack**.

4. On the **Select Template** page, select **Use current template**, and then choose **Next**.

5. On the **Specify Details** page, change the values of **Error Code Blacklisting Parameters** as applicable:
   **Request Threshold**
   Type the new maximum number of requests that can be made per minute without being blocked.
   **WAF Block Period**
   Specify the new value of how long (in minutes) that you want AWS WAF to block the IP address after the number of requests from that IP address exceed the value of **Request Threshold**.

6. On the **Options** page, choose **Next**.

7. On the **Review** page, select the **I acknowledge** check box, and then choose **Update**.

   AWS CloudFormation updates the stack to reflect the new values of the parameters.

## Step 4: (Optional) Test Your Thresholds and IP Rules

To test your solution, you can wait until CloudFront generates a new access log file, or you can simulate this process by uploading a sample access log into the Amazon S3 bucket that you specified for receiving log files.

**To test your thresholds and IP rules**

1. Download the sample CloudFront access log file from the AWS website.

2. Open the Amazon S3 console at https://console.aws.amazon.com/s3/.

3. Choose the Amazon S3 bucket that you're using for CloudFront access logs for this tutorial.

4. Choose **Upload**.

5. Choose **Add Files**, choose the sample access log file, and then choose **Start Upload**.

After the upload finishes, perform the following procedure to confirm that the IP addresses were populated automatically in the AWS WAF **Auto Block** rule. Lambda takes a few seconds to process the log file and update the rule.

**To review IP addresses in the Auto Block rule**

1. Open the AWS WAF console at https://console.aws.amazon.com/waf/.

2. In the navigation pane, choose **Rules**.

3. Choose the **Auto Block** rule.

4. Confirm that the **Auto Block** rule includes an IP match condition that contains IP addresses.

## Step 5: (Optional) Delete Your AWS CloudFormation Stack

If you want to stop blocking IP addresses that submit bad requests, delete the AWS CloudFormation stack that you created in Step 1: Create an AWS CloudFormation Stack for Blocking IP Addresses That Submit Bad Requests. This deletes the AWS resources that AWS CloudFormation created and stops the AWS charges for those resources.

**To delete an AWS CloudFormation stack**

1. Sign in to the AWS Management Console and open the AWS CloudFormation console at https://console.aws.amazon.com/cloudformation.

2. Select the check box for the stack. The default name is **BadBehavingIP**.

3. Choose **Delete Stack**.

4. Choose **Yes, Delete** to confirm.

5. To track the progress of the stack deletion, select the check box for the stack, and then choose the **Events** tab in the bottom pane.

## Related Resources

For AWS WAF samples, including Lambda functions, AWS CloudFormation templates, and SDK usage examples, go to GitHub at https://github.com/awslabs/aws-waf-sample.

# Tutorial: Implementing a DDoS-resistant Website Using AWS Services

This tutorial provides step-by-step instructions for setting up a website that is resistant to distributed denial of service (DDoS) attacks. A DDoS attack can flood your website with traffic, prevent legitimate users from accessing the site, and even cause your site to crash due to the overwhelming traffic volume.

**Topics**

- Overview
- Architecture
- Prerequisites
- Step 1: Launch a Virtual Server Using Amazon EC2
- Step 2: Scale Your Traffic Using Elastic Load Balancing
- Step 3: Improve Performance and Absorb Attacks Using Amazon CloudFront
- Step 4: Register Your Domain Name and Implement DNS Service Using Route 53
- Step 5: Detect and Filter Malicious Web Requests Using AWS WAF
- Additional Best Practices

## Overview

This tutorial shows you how to use several AWS services together to build a resilient, highly secure website. For example, you learn how to do the following:

- Use load balancers and edge servers, which distribute traffic to multiple instances across regions and zones and help to protect your instances from SSL-based attacks
- Mitigate infrastructure (layer 3 and layer 4) DDoS attacks with techniques like overprovisioning your capacity
- Use a web application firewall to monitor HTTP and HTTPS requests and control access to your content

The tutorial shows how to integrate AWS services such as Amazon EC2, Elastic Load Balancing, CloudFront, Route 53, and AWS WAF. Although the tutorial is designed as an end-to-end solution, you don't have to complete every step if you're already using some of those AWS services. For example, if you've already registered your website domain with Route 53 and are using Route 53 as your DNS service, you can skip those steps.

The tutorial is intended to help you launch each AWS service quickly. For that reason, it doesn't cover all possible options. For detailed information about each service, see AWS Documentation. For many of the steps, this tutorial provides specific values to enter. Generally you should use those values. However, in certain cases, such as domain name for your website, use what is appropriate for your needs.

Each main step of the tutorial briefly describes the following:

- What you are doing
- Why you are doing it (that is, how it contributes to your DDoS protection)
- How to do it

**Important**
You are responsible for the cost of the AWS services implemented in this tutorial. For full details, see the pricing webest-practicesage for each AWS service that you use in this solution. You can find links to each service on the Cloud Products page.

## Architecture

The following diagram shows the architecture deployed in this tutorial.

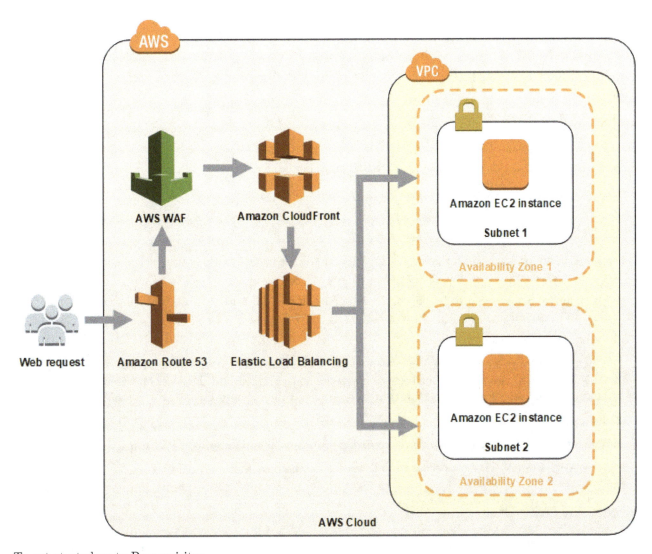

To get started go to Prerequisites.

# Prerequisites

The following tasks are not specifically related to DDoS protection, but are necessary to complete the tutorial.

**Topics**

- Sign Up for AWS
- Create an IAM User
- Create a Key Pair
- Create a Virtual Private Cloud (VPC) with Two Subnets
- Create a Security Group

## Sign Up for AWS

When you sign up for Amazon Web Services (AWS), your AWS account is automatically signed up for all services in AWS. You are charged only for the services that you use.

If you have an AWS account already, skip to the next task. If you don't have an AWS account, use the following procedure to create one.

**To create an AWS account**

1. Open https://aws.amazon.com/, and then choose **Create an AWS Account. Note**
   This might be unavailable in your browser if you previously signed into the AWS Management Console. In that case, choose **Sign in to a different account**, and then choose **Create a new AWS account**.

2. Follow the online instructions.

   Part of the sign-up procedure involves receiving a phone call and entering a PIN using the phone keypad.

Note your AWS account number, because you'll need it for the next task.

## Create an IAM User

To access AWS services and resources, you must provide credentials. Although it's possible to sign in with the user name and password that you created when you first opened your AWS account, for security purposes we strongly recommend that you create new credentials through the AWS Identity and Access Management (IAM) service, and that you use those credentials to sign in.

If you signed up for AWS but have not created an IAM user for yourself, you can create one using the following procedure.

**To create an IAM user for yourself and add the user to an Administrators group**

1. Sign in to the AWS Management Console and open the IAM console at https://console.aws.amazon.com/iam/.

2. In the navigation pane, choose **Users**, and then choose **Add user**.

3. For **User name**, type a user name, such as **Administrator**. The name can consist of letters, digits, and the following characters: plus (+), equal (=), comma (,), period (.), at (@), underscore (_), and hyphen (-). The name is not case sensitive and can be up to 64 characters in length.

4. Select the check box next to **AWS Management Console access**, select **Custom password**, and then type the new user's password in the text box.

5. Choose **Next: Permissions**.

6. On the **Set permissions for user** page, choose **Add user to group**.

7. Choose **Create group**.

8. In the **Create group** dialog box, type the name for the new group. The name can consist of letters, digits, and the following characters: plus (+), equal (=), comma (,), period (.), at (@), underscore (_), and hyphen (-). The name is not case sensitive and can be up to 128 characters in length.

9. For **Filter**, choose **Job function**.

10. In the policy list, select the check box for ** AdministratorAccess**. Then choose **Create group**.

11. Back in the list of groups, select the check box for your new group. Choose **Refresh** if necessary to see the group in the list.

12. Choose **Next: Review** to see the list of group memberships to be added to the new user. When you are ready to proceed, choose **Create user**.

To sign in as this new IAM user, sign out of the AWS console, then use the following URL, where *your_aws_account_id* is your AWS account number without the hyphens (for example, if your AWS account number is 1234-5678-9012, your AWS account ID is 123456789012):

1 `https://your_aws_account_id.signin.aws.amazon.com/console/`

Enter the IAM user name (not your email address) and password that you just created. When you're signed in, the navigation bar displays *"your_user_name @ your_aws_account_id"*.

To verify the sign-in link for IAM users for your account, open the IAM console and check under **IAM users sign-in link** on the dashboard.

For more information about IAM, see the IAM User Guide.

## Create a Key Pair

A *key pair* is a set of security credentials that you use to prove your identity. A key pair consists of a private key and a public key that you create. You use your key pair to log in to your Amazon EC2 instance, which is a virtual server in the AWS Cloud. You specify the name of the key pair when you initially launch the instance.

**To create a key pair**

1. Sign in to AWS using the URL that you created in the previous section.

2. From the AWS dashboard, choose **EC2** to open the Amazon EC2 console.

3. From the navigation bar, select a region for the key pair. You can select any region that's available to you, regardless of your location. However, key pairs are specific to a region; for example, if you plan to launch an instance in the US West (Oregon) Region, you must create a key pair for the instance in the US West (Oregon) Region. For this tutorial, consider choosing the US West (Oregon) Region. **Note**
Later in this tutorial, we use AWS Lambda and Amazon API Gateway, which currently are available only in specific AWS Regions. Therefore, ensure that you select an AWS Region where both Lambda and Amazon API Gateway are available. US West (Oregon), suggested above, supports all the services that are used in this tutorial. For the most current service availability information, see AWS service offerings by region.

4. In the navigation pane, under **NETWORK & SECURITY**, choose **Key Pairs**. **Tip**
The navigation pane is on the left side of the console. If you do not see the pane, it might be minimized; choose the arrow to expand the pane. You might have to scroll down to see the **Key Pairs** link.

5. Choose **Create Key Pair**.

6. Type a name for the new key pair in the **Key pair name** field of the **Create Key Pair** dialog box, and then choose **Create**. Use a name that is easy for you to remember, such as your IAM user name, followed by -key-pair, plus the region name. For example, *me*-key-pair-*uswest2*.

7. The private key file is automatically downloaded by your browser. The base file name is the name that you specified as the name of your key pair, and the file name extension is .pem. Save the private key file in a safe place. **Important**

   This is the only chance for you to save the private key file. You must provide the name of your key pair when you launch an instance and the corresponding private key each time you connect to the instance.

For more information, see Amazon EC2 Key Pairs.

## Create a Virtual Private Cloud (VPC) with Two Subnets

Amazon VPC enables you to launch AWS resources into a virtual network that you've defined. In this tutorial your VPC will contain the two Amazon EC2 instances that host your website along with two subnets connected to those instances.

For more information about Amazon VPC, see What is Amazon VPC? in the *Amazon VPC User Guide*.

### To create a nondefault VPC

1. Open the Amazon VPC console at https://console.aws.amazon.com/vpc/.

2. From the navigation bar, select a region for the VPC. VPCs are specific to a region, so you should select the same region in which you created your key pair. For this tutorial, we use the US West (Oregon) Region.

3. On the VPC dashboard, choose **Start VPC Wizard**.

4. On the **Step 1: Select a VPC Configuration** page, ensure that **VPC with a Single Public Subnet** is selected, and then choose **Select**.

5. On the **Step 2: VPC with a Single Public Subnet** page, specify the following details:

   - For **VPC name**, type a friendly name for your VPC.
   - For **Availability Zone**, choose **us-west-2a**.
   - For **Subnet name**, type subnet-1.
   - Keep the other default configuration settings.

6. Choose **Create VPC**. On the confirmation page, choose **OK**.

### Add a Second Subnet to Your VPC

For increased availability, later in this tutorial you configure a load balancer to use different subnets in two different Availability Zones. When you created your Amazon VPC in the previous step, you created the first subnet in an Availability Zone. You now must add a second subnet in a different Availability Zone. Both Availability Zones must be in the same AWS Region.

### To add a second subnet to your Amazon VPC

1. Open the Amazon VPC console at https://console/.aws/.amazon/.com/vpc//.

2. In the navigation pane, choose **Subnets, Create Subnet**.

3. Specify the following subnet details:

   - For **Name tag**, provide a name for your subnet. For example, type subnet-2. Doing so creates a tag with a key of Name and the value that you specify.
   - For **VPC**, choose the VPC that you just created in the previous steps.
   - For **Availability Zone**, choose an Availability Zone that your subnet will reside in. This should be different than the Availability Zone that you created with your VPC earlier in this tutorial. The tutorial used us-west-2a as an example. So this time, choose something other than us-west-2a, such as us-west-2b.

- For **IPv4 CIDR block**, specify an IPv4 CIDR block for this second subnet. You must specify an IPv4 CIDR block for the subnet from the range of your VPC. The IP addresses for your two subnets cannot overlap. Assuming you used the defaults when setting up your VPC, your first subnet used CIDR block 10.0.0.0/24. So for this second CIDR block, you can use 10.0.1.0/24. For more information, see VPC and Subnet Sizing for IPv4.

4. Choose **Yes, create**.

5. On the subnets page, choose the *first* subnet you created, `subnet-1`.

6. In the details pane, on the **Route Table** tab, note the **Route Table** ID. It starts with **rtb-**.

7. On the subnets page, choose the *second* subnet that you created, `subnet-2`.

8. On the details pane, choose **Edit**.

9. Your second subnet must use the same route table as your first subnet. For **Change to**, select the name of the route table that you noted earlier.

10. Choose **Save**.

## Create a Security Group

Security groups act as a firewall for associated instances, controlling both inbound and outbound traffic at the instance level. You must add rules to a security group that enable you to connect to your instance from your IP address using RDP. You can also add rules that allow inbound and outbound HTTP and HTTPS access from anywhere.

**Prerequisites**

You need the public IPv4 address of your local computer. The security group editor in the Amazon EC2 console can automatically detect the public IPv4 address for you. Alternatively, you can use the search phrase "what is my IP address" in an internet browser. If you are connecting through an internet service provider (ISP) or from behind a firewall without a static IP address, you must find out the range of IP addresses used by client computers.

**To create a security group with least privilege**

1. Open the Amazon EC2 console at https://console.aws.amazon.com/ec2/.

2. From the navigation bar, select a region for the security group. Security groups are specific to a region, so you should select the same region in which you created your key pair, US West (Oregon).

3. In the navigation pane, choose **Security Groups** .

4. Choose **Create Security Group**.

5. Type a name for the new security group and a description. Use a name that is easy for you to remember, such as your IAM user name, followed by _SG_, plus the region name. For example, *me_SG_uswest2*.

6. In the **VPC** list, select the VPC that you created earlier in this tutorial.

7. On the **Inbound** tab, create the following rules (choose **Add Rule** for each new rule):

   - Choose **HTTP** from the **Type** list, and make sure that **Source** is set to **Anywhere** (0.0.0.0/0).
   - Choose **HTTPS** from the **Type** list, and make sure that **Source** is set to **Anywhere** (0.0.0.0/0).
   - Choose **RDP** from the **Type** list. In the **Source** box, choose **MyIP** to automatically populate the field with the public IPv4 address of your local computer. Alternatively, choose **Custom** and specify the public IPv4 address of your computer or network in CIDR notation. To specify an individual IP address in CIDR notation, add the routing suffix /32, for example, 203.0.113.25/32. If your company allocates addresses from a range, specify the entire range, such as 203.0.113.0/24. **Warning**

For security reasons, we don't recommend that you allow RDP access from all IPv4 addresses (0.0.0.0/0) to your instance, except for testing purposes and only for a short time.

8. After you have added all of the rules, choose **Create**.

Next: Step 1: Launch a Virtual Server Using Amazon EC2.

# Step 1: Launch a Virtual Server Using Amazon EC2

You can mitigate infrastructure (layer 3 and layer 4) DDoS attacks by using techniques like overprovisioning capacity. That is, you can scale your website to absorb larger volumes of traffic without capital-intensive investments or unnecessary complexity. You can use Amazon EC2 to launch virtual servers (known as *instances*) and quickly scale up or down as your requirements change. You can scale horizontally by adding instances to your website as needed. You can also choose to scale vertically by using larger instances. In this step of the tutorial, you create a `c4.8xlarge` Amazon EC2 Windows instance, which includes a 10 GB network interface and enhanced networking, in the US West (Oregon) Region.

**Important**
You are responsible for the cost of the AWS services implemented in this tutorial. For full details about EC2 costs, see the Amazon EC2 pricing page.

**Topics**

- Create an Amazon EC2 Instance
- Connect to Your Instance
- Install a Web Server and Host Your Site
- Launch a Second EC2 Instance
- Test Your Website

## Create an Amazon EC2 Instance

The Amazon EC2 instances you create here will host your website.

**To launch an instance**

1. Open the Amazon EC2 console at https://console.aws.amazon.com/ec2/.

2. In the navigation pane, choose the US West (Oregon) Region (or whatever region you chose for your VPC).

3. From the Amazon EC2 dashboard, choose **Launch Instance**.

4. The **Choose an Amazon Machine Image (AMI)** page displays a list of basic configurations, called *Amazon Machine Images (AMIs)*, that serve as templates for your instance. Choose the AMI for **Windows Server 2016 R2 Base**.

5. On the **Choose an Instance Type** page, choose the `c4.8xlarge` type. This type provides a 10 GB network interface and support for enhanced networking.

6. Choose **Review and Launch**.

7. Choose **Edit Instance Details**.

8. For **Network**, choose the VPC that you created in the prerequisites step, Create a Virtual Private Cloud (VPC) with Two Subnets.

9. For **Subnet**, choose **subnet-1**, which you created and named when creating the VPC.

10. For **Auto-assign Public IP**, choose **Enable**.

11. Choose **Review and Launch**.

12. On the **Review Instance Launch** page, under **Security Groups**, use the following steps to choose the security group that you created in the prerequisites step, Create a Security Group.

    1. Choose **Edit security groups**.

    2. On the **Configure Security Group** page, ensure that **Select an existing security group** is selected.

3. Choose the security group that you created earlier from the list of existing security groups, and then choose **Review and Launch**.

13. On the **Review Instance Launch** page, choose **Launch**.

14. When prompted for a key pair, select **Choose an existing key pair**, and then select the key pair that you created in the prerequisites step, Create a Key Pair. **Warning**
Don't select the **Proceed without a key pair** option. If you launch your instance without a key pair, you can't connect to it.

    Select the acknowledgement check box, and then choose **Launch Instances**.

15. A confirmation page lets you know that your instance is launching. Choose **View Instances** to close the confirmation page and return to the console.

16. On the **Instances** page, you can view the status of the launch. It takes a short time for an instance to launch. When you launch an instance, its initial state is `pending`. After the instance starts, its state changes to `running` and it receives a public DNS name. (If the **Public DNS (IPv4)** column is hidden, choose the Show/Hide icon in the top-right corner of the page, and then select **Public DNS (IPv4)**.) Take note of your public IPv4 address. You need this value later in this tutorial.

17. It can take a few minutes for the instance to be ready so that you can connect to it. Check that your instance has passed its status checks; you can view this information in the **Status Checks** column.

## Connect to Your Instance

You will use Microsoft Remote Desktop to connect to your instances. If you are connecting from a Microsoft Windows computer, Remote Desktop is already installed. If you are using another operating system, you might need to install Remote Desktop before performing the following procedure.

**To connect to your Windows instance using an RDP client**

1. In the Amazon EC2 console, select the instance, and then choose **Connect**.

2. In the **Connect To Your Instance** dialog box, choose **Get Password** (it will take a few minutes after the instance is launched before the password is available).

3. Choose **Browse** and navigate to the private key file that you created when you launched the instance. Select the file and choose **Open** to copy the entire contents of the file into the **Contents** field.

4. Choose **Decrypt Password**. The console displays the default administrator password for the instance in the **Connect To Your Instance** dialog box, replacing the link to **Get Password** shown previously with the actual password.

5. Record the default administrator password, or copy it to the clipboard. You need this password to connect to the instance.

6. Choose **Download Remote Desktop File**. Your browser prompts you to either open or save the .rdp file. Either option is fine. When you have finished, you can choose **Close** to dismiss the **Connect To Your Instance** dialog box.

    - If you opened the .rdp file, you see the **Remote Desktop Connection** dialog box.
    - If you saved the .rdp file, navigate to your downloads directory, and then open the .rdp file to display the dialog box.

7. You might get a warning that the publisher of the remote connection is unknown. You can continue to connect to your instance.

8. When prompted, connect to and log in to the instance, using the administrator account for the operating system and the password that you recorded or copied previously. **Note**
Sometimes copying and pasting content can corrupt data. If you encounter a "Password Failed" error when you log in, try typing in the password manually.

9. Due to the nature of self-signed certificates, you might get a warning that the security certificate could not be authenticated. Use the following steps to verify the identity of the remote computer, or simply choose **Yes** or **Continue** to continue if you trust the certificate.

   1. If you are using **Remote Desktop Connection** from a Windows PC, choose **View certificate**. If you are using **Microsoft Remote Desktop** on a Mac, choose **Show Certificate**.

   2. Choose the **Details** tab, and scroll down to the **Thumbest-practicesrint** entry on a Windows PC, or the **SHA1 Fingerprints** entry on a Mac. This is the unique identifier for the remote computer's security certificate.

   3. In the Amazon EC2 console, select the instance, choose **Actions**, and then choose **Get System Log**.

   4. In the system log output, look for an entry labeled `RDPCERTIFICATE-THUMbest-practicesRINT`. If this value matches the thumbest-practicesrint or fingerprint of the certificate, you have verified the identity of the remote computer.

   5. If you are using **Remote Desktop Connection** from a Windows PC, return to the **Certificate** dialog box and choose **OK**. If you are using **Microsoft Remote Desktop** on a Mac, return to the **Verify Certificate** and choose **Continue**.

   6. [Windows] Choose **Yes** in the **Remote Desktop Connection** window to connect to your instance.

      [Mac OS] Log in as prompted, using the default administrator account and the default administrator password that you recorded or copied previously. You might need to switch spaces to see the login screen. For more information about spaces, see http://support.apple.com/kb/PH14155.

   7. If you receive an error while attempting to connect to your instance, see Remote Desktop can't connect to the remote computer.

## Install a Web Server and Host Your Site

The next step is to install a web hosting service on your Amazon EC2 instance and build your website. You have several options for a web server, such as Microsoft Internet Information Server (IIS), which is already part of your instance, Apache HTTP Server for Windows, and others.

Installing a web server and configuring your website is outside the scope of this tutorial. Refer to the proper product documentation to implement a web server on your instance. However, as an example, at a general level, the steps for installing IIS are the following:

- Connect to your instance as described earlier.
- Using Windows Server Manager, choose **Add roles and features**.
- Choose **Role-based or feature-based installation**.
- Choose **Web Server (IIS)** and begin the installation process.
- After the installation is complete, build your website.

## Launch a Second EC2 Instance

You now must repeat this process (launch another EC2 instance and build your website) to create a duplicate of your first EC2 instance. This is necessary to enable load balancing later in the tutorial.

Follow all the same steps just described to launch an instance. Be sure to edit the second instance details and security group as per the previous steps. When editing the instance details, note the following:

- Choose the same VPC as your first instance, the VPC that you created in the prerequisites.
- For **Subnet**, choose **subnet-2**. This is the *second* subnet that you created in the prerequisites step. This is *not* the same subnet that you used for your first instance.
- For **Auto-assign Public IP**, choose **Enable**.

After launching your second Amazon EC2 instance, install the same web hosting service and files as your first EC2 instance.

## Test Your Website

You should now be able to view your website using the public address of each instance.

**To test your Amazon EC2 instances and website**

1. In the Amazon EC2 console, select the check box next to your first instance.

2. In the details pane, note the **Public DNS address**.

3. Enter this address in a web browser. You should be directed to your website.

4. Repeat these steps for the second instance.

Next: Step 2: Scale Your Traffic Using Elastic Load Balancing.

# Step 2: Scale Your Traffic Using Elastic Load Balancing

Elastic Load Balancing provides additional protection against application layer attacks. Elastic Load Balancing distributes traffic to multiple Amazon EC2 instances. Using Elastic Load Balancing, along with CloudFront (discussed later in this tutorial), SSL negotiation is handled by the load balancer and CloudFront edge servers, which helps to protect your Amazon EC2 instances from SSL-based attacks.

**Important**
You are responsible for the cost of the AWS services implemented in this tutorial. For full details about Elastic Load Balancing costs, see the Elastic Load Balancing pricing page.

**Topics**

- Before You Begin
- Create Your Load Balancer
- Test Your Load Balancer

## Before You Begin

Ensure that the Amazon EC2 instances that you launched earlier in this tutorial are in the **Active** state.

## Create Your Load Balancer

Next, you configure a load balancer that automatically routes traffic to your two Amazon EC2 instances.

**To create a load balancer**

1. Open the Amazon EC2 console at https://console.aws.amazon.com/ec2/.

2. On the navigation bar, select the same region that you selected for your EC2 instances.

3. In the navigation pane, under **LOAD BALANCING**, choose **Target Groups**.

4. Choose **Create target group**.

5. Specify a name, protocol, port, and VPC for the target group, and then choose **Create**. For this tutorial, use the following values:

   - **Name**: MyWebServers
   - **Protocol**: HTTP
   - **Port**: 80
   - **Target type**: Instance
   - **VPC**: The VPC that contains your EC2 instances
   - Keep the other settings.

6. Select the new target group.

7. On the **Targets** tab, choose **Edit**.

8. For **Instances**, select both of the instances that you created earlier in this tutorial. Choose **Add to registered**, and then choose **Save**.

   The status of the instances is `initial` until the instances are registered and have passed health checks, and then it is `unused` until you configure the target group to receive traffic from the load balancer.

9. In the navigation pane, under **LOAD BALANCING**, choose **Load Balancers**.

10. Choose **Create Load Balancer**.

11. For **Select load balancer type**, choose **Application Load Balancer**.

12. Choose **Create**.

13. Complete the **Configure Load Balancer** page as follows:

    1. For **Name**, type a name for your load balancer.

    2. For **Scheme**, choose \*\* Internet-facing\*\*. An internet-facing load balancer routes requests from clients over the internet to targets. An internal load balancer routes requests to targets using private IP addresses.

    3. For **Listeners**, the default is a listener that accepts HTTP traffic on port 80.

    4. For **Availability Zones**, select the VPC that you used for your EC2 instances. Select at least two Availability Zones. If there is one subnet for an Availability Zone, it is selected. If there is more than one subnet for an Availability Zone, select one of the subnets. You can select only one subnet per Availability Zone.

    5. Choose **Next: Configure Security Settings**.

14. For now, ignore the message about creating a secure listener group. Choose **Next: Configure Security Groups**.

15. Complete the **Configure Security Groups** page as follows:

    1. Select **Create a new security group**.

    2. Type a name and description for the security group, or keep the default name and description. This new security group contains a rule that allows traffic to the port that you selected for your load balancer on the **Configure Load Balancer** page.

    3. Choose **Next: Configure Routing**.

16. Complete the **Configure Routing** page as follows:

    1. For **Target group**, choose **Existing target group**.

    2. For **Name**, choose the target group that you created earlier.

    3. Choose **Next: Register Targets**.

17. On the **Register Targets** page, the instances that you registered with the target group appear under **Registered instances**. You can't modify the targets registered with the target group until after you complete the wizard. Choose **Next: Review**.

18. On the **Review** page, choose **Create**.

19. After you are notified that your load balancer was created successfully, choose **Close**.

## Test Your Load Balancer

You should now be able to view your website using the DNS name of the load balancer.

**To test your load balancer**

1. On the Amazon EC2 console, in the navigation pane, select **Load Balancers**.

2. Select the box next to your load balancer.

3. In the details pane, note the **DNS name**.

4. Enter this address in a web browser. You should be directed to your website.

**Important**
If you make changes to the website, you must make the same changes to both EC2 instances. The load balancer can serve content from either instance, so it is important that both instances are identical.

Next: Step 3: Improve Performance and Absorb Attacks Using Amazon CloudFront.

# Step 3: Improve Performance and Absorb Attacks Using Amazon CloudFront

Highly scaled, diverse internet connections can significantly improve the response time of your website, better absorb DDoS attacks, and isolate faults. Amazon CloudFront edge servers along with Route 53 provide the additional layer of network infrastructure that you need to achieve these benefits. Your content is served and DNS queries are resolved from locations that typically are closer to your users than your EC2 origin servers. This reduces the load on your origin EC2 servers.

**Important**
You are responsible for the cost of the AWS services implemented in this tutorial. For full details about CloudFront costs, see the CloudFront pricing page.

**Topics**

- Deliver Your Content Using Amazon CloudFront

## Deliver Your Content Using Amazon CloudFront

Amazon CloudFront is a content delivery network (CDN) service that you can use to deliver your entire website, including static, dynamic, streaming, and interactive content. You can use persistent TCP connections and variable time-to-live (TTL) to accelerate the delivery of your content, even if it can't be cached at an edge location. This allows you to use CloudFront to protect your web application, even if you are not serving static content.

CloudFront accepts only well-formed connections to prevent many common DDoS attacks, like SYN floods and UDP reflection attacks, from reaching your origin. CloudFront can automatically close connections that are unusually slow, which can indicate a potential DDoS attack.

Further, DDoS attacks are geographically isolated close to the source, which prevents the traffic from affecting other locations. You can also use the CloudFront geo restriction feature to prevent users in specific geographic locations from accessing your content. This can be useful in case you want to block attacks that are originating from geographic locations where you do not expect to serve users.

All of these capabilities can greatly improve your ability to continue serving traffic to users during large DDoS attacks.

**To implement Amazon CloudFront**

1. Open the CloudFront console at https://console.aws.amazon.com/cloudfront/.

2. Choose **Create Distribution**.

3. On the **Select a delivery method for your content** page, in the **Web** section, choose **Get Started**.

4. On the **Create Distribution** page, for **Origin name**, type the name of the load balancer that you created earlier in the tutorial. To find the name, go to the Amazon EC2 dashboard and choose **Load Balancers** in the navigation pane. Choose the load balancer that you created earlier.

5. Accept all the default values for the remainder of the **Origin Settings** fields.

6. Under **Default Cache Behavior Settings**, accept the default values, and CloudFront will do the following:

    - Forward all requests that use the CloudFront URL for your distribution (for example, `http://d111111abcdef8.cloudfront.net/image.jpg`) to the load balancer that you specified earlier
    - Allow users to use either HTTP or HTTPS to access your objects
    - Respond to requests for your objects
    - Cache your objects at CloudFront edge locations for 24 hours

- Forward only the default request headers to your origin and not cache your objects based on the values in the headers
- Allow everyone to view your content
- Not automatically compress your content

For more information, see Cache Behavior Settings.

7. Under **Distribution Settings**, accept the defaults, other than the following:
   **Price Class**
   Select the price class that corresponds with the maximum price that you want to pay for CloudFront service. By default, CloudFront serves your objects from edge locations in all CloudFront regions.
   For more information about price classes and about how your choice of price class affects CloudFront performance for your distribution, see Choosing the Price Class for a CloudFront Distribution. For information about CloudFront pricing, including how price classes map to CloudFront regions, see Amazon CloudFront Pricing.
   **AWS WAF Web ACL**
   Choose **None**. You configure AWS WAF later in this tutorial.
   **Alternate Domain Names (CNAMEs) (Optional)**
   Specify a domain name that you want to use for your website's URLs. For example, you could enter `example.com`.
   **Default Root Object (Optional)**
   The object that you want CloudFront to request from your origin (for example, `index.html`) when a viewer requests the root URL of your distribution (`http://example.com/`) instead of an object in your distribution (`http://example.com/product-description.html`). Specifying a default root object avoids exposing the contents of your distribution.
   **Comment (Optional)**
   Enter any comments that you want to save with the distribution.

8. Choose **Create Distribution**.

9. After CloudFront creates your distribution, the value of the **Status** column for your distribution changes from **InProgress** to **Deployed**. If you chose to enable the distribution, it will then be ready to process requests. This should take less than 15 minutes.

   The domain name that CloudFront assigns to your distribution appears in the list of distributions. (It also appears on the **General** tab for a selected distribution.) Note both this name and the Distribution ID because you need these later in the tutorial.

10. On the CloudFront console, note the ID of the distribution that you just created. You need this ID later in the tutorial.

**To test your CloudFront distribution**

1. On the CloudFront console, select the ID of the distribution that you just created. This opens the details page for this distribution. Note the domain name.

2. Open that domain name in a browser. You should see your website. It might take about 15 minutes or so for the distribution to be active. If you get an error that indicates that your origin closed the connection, give it some more time and try again. You might also have to refresh the page in your browser.

Next: Step 4: Register Your Domain Name and Implement DNS Service Using Route 53.

# Step 4: Register Your Domain Name and Implement DNS Service Using Route 53

You can use Route 53 to register the domain name for your website, route internet traffic to the resources for your domain, and check the health of your web server to verify that it's reachable, available, and functional. Route 53 helps to protect against DDoS attacks by providing redundancy and load balancing across multiple DNS servers. Route 53 can also detect anomalies in DNS queries and prioritize requests from users that are known to be reliable and, by extension, deprioritize requests that are from potentially less reliable sources.

**Important**
You are responsible for the cost of the AWS services implemented in this tutorial. For full details about Route 53 costs, see the Route 53 pricing page.

**Topics**

- Register Your Domain with Route 53
- Create Records

## Register Your Domain with Route 53

If you are new to hosting a website, your next step in this tutorial is to register a domain using Route 53. Following are the steps to do this.

**Important**
If your domain is already registered with another registrar, you must migrate your existing domain from the other registrar's DNS service to instead use Route 53 as the DNS service. This tutorial does not cover that transfer process. Instead of following the Route 53 procedures described in this tutorial, you must perform four steps to transfer an existing domain:
Create a hosted zone Get your current DNS configuration from your DNS service provider Create resource records sets Update your registrar's name servers For more information about transferring an existing domain registration from another registrar, see Transferring Domains.

**To register a new domain using Route 53**

1. Sign in to the AWS Management Console and open the Route 53 console at https://console.aws.amazon.com/route53/.

2. Under **Domain Registration**, choose **Get Started Now**.

3. Choose **Register Domain**.

4. Type the domain name that you want to register, and choose **Check** to find out whether the domain name is available. As an example, this tutorial assumes that you register the domain name `example.com`.

   For information about how to specify characters other than a-z, 0-9, and - (hyphen) and how to specify internationalized domain names, see DNS Domain Name Format.

5. If the domain is available, choose **Add to cart**. The domain name appears in your shopping cart.

6. In the shopping cart, choose the number of years that you want to register the domain for.

7. To register more domains, repeat steps 4 through 6.

8. Choose **Continue**.

9. On the **Contact Details for Your** $n$ **Domains** page, enter contact information for the domain registrant, administrator, and technical contacts. The values that you enter here are applied to all the domains that you're registering.

10. For some top-level domains (TLDs), we're required to collect additional information. For these TLDs, enter the applicable values after the **Postal/Zip Code** field.

11. Choose whether you want to hide your contact information from WHOIS queries. For more information, see the following topics:

    - Enabling or Disabling Privacy Protection for Contact Information for a Domain
    - Domains That You Can Register with Route 53

12. Choose **Continue**.

13. Review the information that you entered, read the terms of service, and select the check box to confirm that you've read the terms of service.

14. Choose **Complete Purchase**.

    For generic TLDs, we typically send an email to the registrant for the domain to verify that the registrant contact can be reached at the email address that you specified. (We don't send an email if we already have confirmation that the email address is valid.) The email comes from one of the following email addresses:

    - **noreply@registrar.amazon.com** – for TLDs registered by Amazon Registrar.
    - **noreply@domainnameverification.net** – for TLDs registered by our registrar associate, Gandi. To determine who the registrar is for your TLD, see Domains That You Can Register with Route 53.
    **Important**
    The registrant contact must follow the instructions in the email to verify that the email was received, or we must suspend the domain as required by ICANN. When a domain is suspended, it's not accessible on the internet.

    For all TLDs, you receive an email when your domain registration has been approved. To determine the current status of your request, see Viewing the Status of a Domain Registration.

## Create Records

Your next step is to create records that tell Route 53 how you want to route traffic for the domain and subdomain.

**To create records**

1. Sign in to the AWS Management Console and open the Route 53 console at https://console.aws.amazon.com/route53/.

2. In the navigation pane, choose **Hosted zones**.

3. Because you registered your domain using Route 53, Route 53 automatically creates a hosted zone for you. Choose this hosted zone.

4. Choose **Create Record Set**.

5. Enter the applicable values:

    - For **Name**, leave as is (it should already be example.com).
    - For **Type**, choose **A – IPv4 address**.
    - For **Alias**, choose **Yes**.
    - For **Alias Target**, type the domain name of your CloudFront distribution that you created earlier in this tutorial.

6. Choose **Create**.

**Note**
Your new record takes time to propagate to the Route 53 DNS servers. Changes generally propagate to all Route 53 name servers within 60 seconds.

**To test your Route 53 records**

1. Open the domain name you added to the record, such as example.com, in a browser.

2. You should see your website.

Next: Step 5: Detect and Filter Malicious Web Requests Using AWS WAF.

# Step 5: Detect and Filter Malicious Web Requests Using AWS WAF

You can use a web application firewall (WAF) to protect your web applications against attacks that attempt to exploit a vulnerability in your website. Common examples include SQL injection or cross-site request forgery. You can also use a firewall to detect and mitigate web application layer DDoS attacks.

AWS WAF is a web application firewall service that lets you monitor the HTTP and HTTPS requests that are forwarded to Amazon CloudFront or an Application Load Balancer. AWS WAF also lets you control access to your content. Based on conditions that you specify, such as the IP addresses that requests originate from or the values of query strings, CloudFront responds to the requests either with the requested content or with an HTTP 403 status code (Forbidden).

Some attacks consist of web traffic that is disguised to look like regular user traffic. To mitigate this type of attack, you can use AWS WAF rate-based blacklisting. With rate-based blacklisting, you can set a threshold for how many requests your web application can serve. If a bot or crawler exceeds this limit, you can use AWS WAF to automatically block any additional requests.

AWS provides preconfigured templates that include a set of AWS WAF rules, which you can customize to best fit your needs. These templates are designed to block common web-based attacks such as bad bots, SQL injection, cross-site scripting (XSS), HTTP floods, and known-attacker attacks. This tutorial uses these templates to provide firewall protection for your website. The following procedures show you how to deploy the templates using AWS CloudFormation. For more information, including an diagram of the template's solution, see AWS WAF Security Automations.

The template uses some AWS features, such as AWS Lambda and Amazon API Gateway, that are not covered in this tutorial. The template performs all the necessary configuration, so you don't need to perform any additional actions for those services. However, if you want to learn more about Lambda and Amazon API Gateway, see the AWS Lambda Developer Guide and Amazon API Gateway Developer Guide.

**Important**
You are responsible for the cost of all the AWS services that are deployed as part of this template, including Amazon S3, AWS Lambda, Amazon API Gateway, AWS WAF, and others. For full details, see the pricing page for each AWS service.

**Topics**

- Launch the Stack (Template)
- Associate the Web ACL with Your Web Application
- Configure Web Access Logging

## Launch the Stack (Template)

This automated AWS CloudFormation template deploys the AWS WAF Security Automations solution on the AWS Cloud.

**To launch the AWS CloudFormation stack (template)**

1. Sign into the AWS CloudFormation console.

2. If this is your first time using AWS CloudFormation, on the **Select Template** page, choose **Specify an Amazon S3 template URL** and then enter https://s3/.amazonaws/.com/solutions/-reference/aws/-waf/-security/-automations/latest/aws/-waf/-security/-automations/.template/. If you've used AWS CloudFormation in the past, choose **Create stack**, and then choose **Specify an Amazon S3 template URL** and enter https://s3/.amazonaws/.com/solutions/-reference/aws/-waf/-security/-automations/latest/aws/-waf/-security/-automations/.template/.

3. Choose **Next**.

4. On the **Specify Details** page, specify the following values:

**Stack Name**

Type a name for the AWS WAF configuration. This will also be the name of the web ACL that the template creates, for example, `MyWebsiteACL`.

**Activate SQL Injection Protection**

Choose **yes** to enable the component that is designed to block common SQL injection attacks.

**Activate Cross-site Scripting Protection**

Choose **yes** to enable the component that is designed to block common XSS attacks.

**Activate HTTP Flood Protection**

Choose **no**. The rate-based rules provided by AWS WAF are a more efficient way to set up this protection. After completing this tutorial, if you want to add rate-based rules, you can find more information in How AWS WAF Works.

**Activate Scanner & Probe Protection**

Choose **yes** to enable the component that is designed to block scanners and probes.

**Activate Reputation List Protection**

Choose **yes** to block requests from IP addresses on third-party reputation lists (supported lists: spamhaus, torproject, and emergingthreats).

**Activate Bad Bot Protection**

Choose **yes**. The template requires this protection to be enabled. However, to take full advantage of this protection, you must complete additional steps outside the scope of this tutorial, such as creating a honeypot link. Those steps are described AWS WAF Security Automations, Step 3. Embed the Honeypot Link in Your Web Application. These additional steps are optional and are not required to complete this tutorial. If you choose to perform these additional steps, complete this tutorial first, and then you can set up the honeypot link.

**CloudFront Access Log Bucket Name**

Type a name for the Amazon S3 bucket where you want to store access logs for your CloudFront distribution. This is the name of a new bucket that the template creates during stack launch. Do not use an existing name.

**Request Threshold**

This is used for the HTTP flood protection, so is not applicable for this tutorial. You can leave the default, which is 400.

**Error Threshold**

Type 50. This is the maximum acceptable bad requests per minute per IP address. This is used by the scanner and probe protection.

**WAF Block Period**

Type 240. This is the period (in minutes) to block applicable IP addresses that are identified by the scanner and probe protection.

**Send Anonymous Usage Data**

Choose **yes** to send anonymous data to AWS to help us understand solution usage across our customer base as a whole. To opt out of this feature, choose **no**.

5. Choose **Next**.

6. Make no changes on the **Options** page.

7. Choose **Next**.

8. On the **Review** page, review and confirm the settings. Be sure to select the check box acknowledging that the template will create AWS Identity and Access Management (IAM) resources.

9. Choose **Create** to deploy the stack.

You can view the status of the stack in the AWS CloudFormation console in the **Status** column. You should see a status of **CREATE_COMPLETE** in about fifteen (15) minutes.

## Associate the Web ACL with Your Web Application

Now associate your Amazon CloudFront web distribution with the web ACL.

**To associate the web ACL with your web application**

1. Sign in to the AWS Management Console and open the AWS WAF console at https://console.aws.amazon.com/waf/.

2. In the navigation pane, choose **Web ACLs**.

3. Select your newly created WebACL. The name of this ACL is the name that you specified in the previous step, for example, `MyWebsiteACL`.

4. Choose the **Rules** tab.

5. Choose **Add association**.

6. For **AWS resources using this web ACL**, choose the CloudFront distribution that you created earlier in this tutorial.

7. Choose **Add** to save your changes.

## Configure Web Access Logging

As the last step of this tutorial, you configure Amazon CloudFront to send web access logs to the appropriate Amazon S3 bucket so that this data is available for the Log Parser AWS Lambda function.

**To store web access logs from a CloudFront distribution**

1. Open the Amazon CloudFront console at https://console.aws.amazon.com/cloudfront/.

2. Choose the check box next to your distribution, and then choose **Distribution Settings**.

3. On the **General** tab, choose **Edit**.

4. Confirm that for **AWS WAF Web ACL**, the web ACL that the solution created (the same name that you assigned to the stack during initial configuration) is already entered.

5. For **Logging**, choose **On**.

6. For **Bucket for Logs**, choose the Amazon S3 bucket that you want use to store web access logs (that you defined in Launch the Stack (Template)).

7. Choose **Yes, edit** to save your changes.

Next: Additional Best Practices.

# Additional Best Practices

You now have several components in place to help protect your website from DDoS attacks. However, there is still more you can do. Following are several best practices you should consider. This tutorial does not cover the implementation details of the best practices, but links to relevant documentation are provided.

**Topics**

- Obscuring AWS Resources
- Using Security Groups
- Network Access Control Lists (ACLs)
- Protecting Your Origin
- Conclusion

## Obscuring AWS Resources

For many website applications, your AWS resources do not need to be fully exposed to the internet. For example, it might not be necessary for Amazon EC2 instances behind an elastic load balancer (ELB) to be publicly accessible. In this scenario, you might decide to allow users to access the ELB on certain TCP ports and to allow only the ELB to communicate with the Amazon EC2 instances. You can do this by configuring security groups and network access control lists (ACLs) within your Amazon Virtual Private Cloud (VPC). Amazon VPC allows you to provision a logically isolated section of the AWS Cloud where you can launch AWS resources in a virtual network that you define.

Security groups and network ACLs are similar in that they allow you to control access to AWS resources within your Amazon VPC. Security groups allow you to control inbound and outbound traffic at the instance level. Network ACLs offer similar capabilities, but at the VPC subnet level. Additionally, there is no charge for inbound data transfer on Amazon EC2 security group rules or network ACLs. This ensures that you do not incur any additional charges for traffic that is dropped by your security groups or network ACLs.

## Using Security Groups

You can specify security groups when launching an Amazon EC2 instance or associate the instance with a security group later on. All traffic to a security group from the internet is implicitly denied unless you create an `Allow` rule to permit the traffic. For example, in this tutorial, you created a solution that consists of an ELB and two Amazon EC2 instances. You should consider creating one security group for the ELB ("ELB security group") and one for the instances ("web application server security group"). You can then create `Allow` rules to permit traffic from the internet to the ELB security group and to permit traffic from the ELB security group to the web application server security group. As a result, traffic from the internet is unable to directly communicate with your Amazon EC2 instances, which makes it more difficult for an attacker to learn about the design and structure of your website.

## Network Access Control Lists (ACLs)

With network ACLs, you can specify both `Allow` and `Deny` rules. This is useful in case you want to explicitly deny certain types of traffic to your website. For example, you can define IP addresses (as CIDR ranges), protocols, and destination ports that should be denied for the entire subnet. If your website is used only for TCP traffic, you can create a rule to deny all UDP traffic, or vice versa. This tool is useful when responding to DDoS attacks because it can allow you to create your own rules to mitigate the attack if you know the source IP addresses or other signature. You can use network ACLs in conjunction with AWS WAF ACLs.

## Protecting Your Origin

You should consider configuring CloudFront to prevent users from bypassing CloudFront and requesting content directly from your origin. This can improve the security of your origin. To learn more, see Using Custom Headers to Restrict Access to Your Content on a Custom Origin.

## Conclusion

The best practices outlined in this tutorial can help you to build a DDoS-resilient architecture that can protect the availability of your website against many common infrastructure and application layer DDoS attacks. The degree to which you are able to architect your application according to these best practices influences the type and volume of DDoS attacks that you can mitigate.

For more information, see the following:

- AWS Best Practices for DDoS Resiliency
- AWS Documentation

# Blog Tutorials

**Blog Tutorials**

The following tutorial topics link out to the AWS Security Blog.

- How to Import IP Address Reputation Lists to Automatically Update AWS WAF IP Blacklists
- How to Reduce Security Threats and Operating Costs Using AWS WAF and Amazon CloudFront
- How to Prevent Hotlinking by Using AWS WAF, Amazon CloudFront, and Referer Checking
- How to Use AWS CloudFormation to Automate Your AWS WAF Configuration with Example Rules and Match Conditions

# Creating and Configuring a Web Access Control List (Web ACL)

A web access control list (web ACL) gives you fine-grained control over the web requests that your Amazon CloudFront distributions or Application Load Balancers respond to. You can allow or block the following types of requests:

- Originate from an IP address or a range of IP addresses
- Originate from a specific country or countries
- Contain a specified string or match a regular expression (regex) pattern in a particular part of requests
- Exceed a specified length
- Appear to contain malicious SQL code (known as SQL injection)
- Appear to contain malicious scripts (known as cross-site scripting)

You can also test for any combination of these conditions, or block or count web requests that not only meet the specified conditions, but also exceed a specified number of requests in any 5-minute period.

To choose the requests that you want to allow to have access to your content or that you want to block, perform the following tasks:

1. Choose the default action, allow or block, for web requests that don't match any of the conditions that you specify. For more information, see Deciding on the Default Action for a Web ACL.

2. Specify the conditions under which you want to allow or block requests:

    - To allow or block requests based on whether the requests appear to contain malicious scripts, create cross-site scripting match conditions. For more information, see Working with Cross-site Scripting Match Conditions.
    - To allow or block requests based on the IP addresses that they originate from, create IP match conditions. For more information, see Working with IP Match Conditions.
    - To allow or block requests based on the country that they originate from, create geo match conditions. For more information, see Working with Geographic Match Conditions.
    - To allow or block requests based on whether the requests exceed a specified length, create size constraint conditions. For more information, see Working with Size Constraint Conditions.
    - To allow or block requests based on whether the requests appear to contain malicious SQL code, create SQL injection match conditions. For more information, see Working with SQL Injection Match Conditions.
    - To allow or block requests based on strings that appear in the requests, create string match conditions. For more information, see Working with String Match Conditions.
    - To allow or block requests based on a regex pattern that appear in the requests, create regex match conditions. For more information, see Working with Regex Match Conditions.

3. Add the conditions to one or more rules. If you add more than one condition to the same rule, web requests must match all the conditions for AWS WAF to allow or block requests based on the rule. For more information, see Working with Rules. Optionally, also add a rate limit to the rule, which specifies the maximum number of requests that are allowed from a specific IP address.

4. Add the rules to a web ACL. For each rule, specify whether you want AWS WAF to allow or block requests based on the conditions that you added to the rule. If you add more than one rule to a web ACL, AWS WAF evaluates the rules in the order that they're listed in the web ACL. For more information, see Working with Web ACLs.

**Topics**

- Working with conditions
- Working with Rules
- Working with Web ACLs

# Working with conditions

Conditions specify when you want to allow or block requests.

- To allow or block requests based on whether the requests appear to contain malicious scripts, create cross-site scripting match conditions. For more information, see Working with Cross-site Scripting Match Conditions.
- To allow or block requests based on the IP addresses that they originate from, create IP match conditions. For more information, see Working with IP Match Conditions.
- To allow or block requests based on the country that they originate from, create geo match conditions. For more information, see Working with Geographic Match Conditions.
- To allow or block requests based on whether the requests exceed a specified length, create size constraint conditions. For more information, see Working with Size Constraint Conditions.
- To allow or block requests based on whether the requests appear to contain malicious SQL code, create SQL injection match conditions. For more information, see Working with SQL Injection Match Conditions.
- To allow or block requests based on strings that appear in the requests, create string match conditions. For more information, see Working with String Match Conditions.
- To allow or block requests based on a regex pattern that appear in the requests, create regex match conditions. For more information, see Working with Regex Match Conditions.

**Topics**

- Working with Cross-site Scripting Match Conditions
- Working with IP Match Conditions
- Working with Geographic Match Conditions
- Working with Size Constraint Conditions
- Working with SQL Injection Match Conditions
- Working with String Match Conditions
- Working with Regex Match Conditions

# Working with Cross-site Scripting Match Conditions

Attackers sometimes insert scripts into web requests in an effort to exploit vulnerabilities in web applications. You can create one or more cross-site scripting match conditions to identify the parts of web requests, such as the URI or the query string, that you want AWS WAF to inspect for possible malicious scripts. Later in the process, when you create a web ACL, you specify whether to allow or block requests that appear to contain malicious scripts.

**Topics**

- Creating Cross-site Scripting Match Conditions
- Values That You Specify When You Create or Edit Cross-site Scripting Match Conditions
- Adding and Deleting Filters in a Cross-site Scripting Match Condition
- Deleting Cross-site Scripting Match Conditions

## Creating Cross-site Scripting Match Conditions

When you create cross-site scripting match conditions, you specify filters. The filters indicate the part of web requests that you want AWS WAF to inspect for malicious scripts, such as the URI or the query string. You can add more than one filter to a cross-site scripting match condition, or you can create a separate condition for each filter. Here's how each configuration affects AWS WAF behavior:

- **More than one filter per cross-site scripting match condition (recommended)** – When you add a cross-site scripting match condition that contains multiple filters to a rule and add the rule to a web ACL, a web request must match only one of the filters in the cross-site scripting match condition for AWS WAF to allow or block the request based on that condition.

  For example, suppose you create one cross-site scripting match condition, and the condition contains two filters. One filter instructs AWS WAF to inspect the URI for malicious scripts, and the other instructs AWS WAF to inspect the query string. AWS WAF allows or blocks requests if they appear to contain malicious scripts *either* in the URI *or* in the query string.

- **One filter per cross-site scripting match condition** – When you add the separate cross-site scripting match conditions to a rule and add the rule to a web ACL, web requests must match all the conditions for AWS WAF to allow or block requests based on the conditions.

  Suppose you create two conditions, and each condition contains one of the two filters in the preceding example. When you add both conditions to the same rule and add the rule to a web ACL, AWS WAF allows or blocks requests only when both the URI and the query string appear to contain malicious scripts.

**Note**
When you add a cross-site scripting match condition to a rule, you also can configure AWS WAF to allow or block web requests that *do not* appear to contain malicious scripts.

**To create a cross-site scripting match condition**

1. Sign in to the AWS Management Console and open the AWS WAF console at https://console.aws.amazon.com/waf/.

2. In the navigation pane, choose **Cross-site scripting**.

3. Choose **Create condition**.

4. Specify the applicable filter settings. For more information, see Values That You Specify When You Create or Edit Cross-site Scripting Match Conditions.

5. Choose **Add another filter**.

6. If you want to add another filter, repeat steps 4 and 5.

7. When you're done adding filters, choose **Create**.

## Values That You Specify When You Create or Edit Cross-site Scripting Match Conditions

When you create or update a cross-site scripting match condition, you specify the following values:

**Name**
The name of the cross-site scripting match condition.
The name can contain only the characters A-Z, a-z, 0-9, and the special characters: _-!"#'+*},./ . You can't change the name of a condition after you create it.

**Part of the request to filter on**
Choose the part of each web request that you want AWS WAF to inspect for malicious scripts:
**Header**
A specified request header, for example, the `User-Agent` or `Referer` header. If you choose **Header**, specify the name of the header in the **Header** field.
**HTTP method**
The HTTP method, which indicates the type of operation that the request is asking the origin to perform. CloudFront supports the following methods: `DELETE`, `GET`, `HEAD`, `OPTIONS`, `PATCH`, `POST`, and `PUT`.
**Query string**
The part of a URL that appears after a ? character, if any.
**URI**
The part of a URL that identifies a resource, for example, `/images/daily-ad.jpg`. Unless a **Transformation** is specified, a URI is not normalized and is inspected just as AWS receives it from the client as part of the request. A **Transformation** will reformat the URI as specified.
**Body**
The part of a request that contains any additional data that you want to send to your web server as the HTTP request body, such as data from a form.
If you choose **Body** for the value of **Part of the request to filter on**, AWS WAF inspects only the first 8192 bytes (8 KB). To allow or block requests for which the body is longer than 8192 bytes, you can create a size constraint condition. (AWS WAF gets the length of the body from the request headers.) For more information, see Working with Size Constraint Conditions.
**Single query parameter (value only)**
Any parameter that you have defined as part of the query string. For example, if the URL is "www.xyz.com?User-Name=abc&SalesRegion=seattle" you can add a filter to either the *UserName* or *SalesRegion* parameter.
If you choose **Single query parameter (value only)**, you will also specify a **Query parameter name**. This is the parameter in the query string that you will inspect, such as *UserName* or *SalesRegion*. The maximum length for **Query parameter name** is 30 characters. **Query parameter name** is not case sensitive. For example, it you specify *UserName* as the **Query parameter name**, this will match all variations of *UserName*, such as *username* and *UsERName*.
**All query parameters (values only)**
Similar to **Single query parameter (value only)**, but rather than inspecting the values of a single parameter, AWS WAF inspects all parameter values within the query string for possible malicious scripts. For example, if the URL is "www.xyz.com?UserName=abc&SalesRegion=seattle," and you choose **All query parameters (values only)**, AWS WAF will trigger a match if either the value of *UserName* or *SalesRegion* contain possible malicious scripts.

**Header**
If you chose **Header** for **Part of the request to filter on**, choose a header from the list of common headers, or type the name of a header that you want AWS WAF to inspect for malicious scripts.

**Transformation**
A transformation reformats a web request before AWS WAF inspects the request. This eliminates some of the unusual formatting that attackers use in web requests in an effort to bypass AWS WAF.

You can only specify a single type of text transformation.

Transformations can perform the following operations:

**None**

AWS WAF doesn't perform any text transformations on the web request before inspecting it for the string in **Value to match**.

**Convert to lowercase**

AWS WAF converts uppercase letters (A-Z) to lowercase (a-z).

**HTML decode**

AWS WAF replaces HTML-encoded characters with unencoded characters:

- Replaces &quot; with &
- Replaces   with a non-breaking space
- Replaces &lt; with <
- Replaces &gt; with >
- Replaces characters that are represented in hexadecimal format, &#xhhhh;, with the corresponding characters
- Replaces characters that are represented in decimal format, &#nnnn;, with the corresponding characters

  **Normalize whitespace**

  AWS WAF replaces the following characters with a space character (decimal 32):

- \f, formfeed, decimal 12
- \t, tab, decimal 9
- \n, newline, decimal 10
- \r, carriage return, decimal 13
- \v, vertical tab, decimal 11
- non-breaking space, decimal 160 In addition, this option replaces multiple spaces with one space.

  **Simplify command line**

  For requests that contain operating system command line commands, use this option to perform the following transformations:

- Delete the following characters: \ " ' ^
- Delete spaces before the following characters: / (
- Replace the following characters with a space: , ;
- Replace multiple spaces with one space
- Convert uppercase letters (A-Z) to lowercase (a-z)

  **URL decode**

  Decode a URL-encoded request.

## Adding and Deleting Filters in a Cross-site Scripting Match Condition

You can add or delete filters in a cross-site scripting match condition. To change a filter, add a new one and delete the old one.

**To add or delete filters in a cross-site scripting match condition**

1. Sign in to the AWS Management Console and open the AWS WAF console at https://console.aws.amazon.com/waf/.

2. In the navigation pane, choose **Cross-site scripting**.

3. Choose the condition that you want to add or delete filters in.

4. To add filters, perform the following steps:

   1. Choose **Add filter**.

   2. Specify the applicable filter settings. For more information, see Values That You Specify When You Create or Edit Cross-site Scripting Match Conditions.

   3. Choose **Add**.

5. To delete filters, perform the following steps:

    1. Select the filter that you want to delete.

    2. Choose **Delete filter**.

## Deleting Cross-site Scripting Match Conditions

If you want to delete a cross-site scripting match condition, you must first delete all filters in the condition and remove the condition from all the rules that are using it, as described in the following procedure.

**To delete a cross-site scripting match condition**

1. Sign in to the AWS Management Console and open the AWS WAF console at https://console.aws.amazon.com/waf/.

2. In the navigation pane, choose **Cross-site scripting**.

3. In the **Cross-site scripting match conditions** pane, choose the cross-site scripting match condition that you want to delete.

4. In the right pane, choose the **Associated rules** tab.

   If the list of rules using this cross-site scripting match condition is empty, go to step 6. If the list contains any rules, make note of the rules, and continue with step 5.

5. To remove the cross-site scripting match condition from the rules that are using it, perform the following steps:

    1. In the navigation pane, choose **Rules**.

    2. Choose the name of a rule that is using the cross-site scripting match condition that you want to delete.

    3. In the right pane, select the cross-site scripting match condition that you want to remove from the rule, and choose **Remove selected condition**.

    4. Repeat steps b and c for all the remaining rules that are using the cross-site scripting match condition that you want to delete.

    5. In the navigation pane, choose **Cross-site scripting**.

    6. In the **Cross-site scripting match conditions** pane, choose the cross-site scripting match condition that you want to delete.

6. Choose **Delete** to delete the selected condition.

# Working with IP Match Conditions

If you want to allow or block web requests based on the IP addresses that the requests originate from, create one or more IP match conditions. An IP match condition lists up to 10,000 IP addresses or IP address ranges that your requests originate from. Later in the process, when you create a web ACL, you specify whether to allow or block requests from those IP addresses.

**Topics**

- Creating an IP Match Condition
- Editing IP Match Conditions
- Deleting IP Match Conditions

## Creating an IP Match Condition

If you want to allow some web requests and block others based on the IP addresses that the requests originate from, create an IP match condition for the IP addresses that you want to allow and another IP match condition for the IP addresses that you want to block.

**Note**
When you add an IP match condition to a rule, you also can configure AWS WAF to allow or block web requests that *do not* originate from the IP addresses that you specify in the condition.

**To create an IP match condition**

1. Sign in to the AWS Management Console and open the AWS WAF console at https://console.aws.amazon.com/waf/.

2. In the navigation pane, choose **IP addresses**.

3. Choose **Create condition**.

4. Type a name in the **Name** field.

   The name can contain only alphanumeric characters (A-Z, a-z, 0-9) or the following special characters: _-!"#'+*},./ . You can't change the name of a condition after you create it.

5. Select the correct IP version and specify an IP address or range of IP addresses by using CIDR notation. Here are some examples:

   - To specify the IPv4 address 192.0.2.44, type **192.0.2.44/32**.
   - To specify the IPv6 address 0:0:0:0:0:ffff:c000:22c, type **0:0:0:0:0:ffff:c000:22c/128**.
   - To specify the range of IPv4 addresses from 192.0.2.0 to 192.0.2.255, type **192.0.2.0/24**.
   - To specify the range of IPv6 addresses from 2620:0:2d0:200:0:0:0:0 to 2620:0:2d0:200:ffff:ffff:ffff:ffff, type **2620:0:2d0:200::/64**.

   AWS WAF supports IPv4 address ranges: /8 and any range between /16 through /32. AWS WAF supports IPv6 address ranges: /16, /24, /32, /48, /56, /64, and /128. For more information about CIDR notation, see the Wikipedia entry Classless Inter-Domain Routing.

6. Choose **Add another IP address or range**.

7. If you want to add another IP address or range, repeat steps 5 and 6.

8. When you're finished adding values, choose **Create IP match condition**.

## Editing IP Match Conditions

You can add an IP address range to an IP match condition or delete a range. To change a range, add a new one and delete the old one.

**To edit an IP match condition**

1. Sign in to the AWS Management Console and open the AWS WAF console at https://console.aws.amazon.com/waf/.

2. In the navigation pane, choose **IP addresses**.

3. In the **IP match conditions** pane, choose the IP match condition that you want to edit.

4. To add an IP address range:

   1. In the right pane, choose **Add IP address or range**.

   2. Select the correct IP version and type an IP address range by using CIDR notation. Here are some examples:

      - To specify the IPv4 address 192.0.2.44, type **192.0.2.44/32**.
      - To specify the IPv6 address 0:0:0:0:0:ffff:c000:22c, type **0:0:0:0:0:ffff:c000:22c/128**.
      - To specify the range of IPv4 addresses from 192.0.2.0 to 192.0.2.255, type **192.0.2.0/24**.
      - To specify the range of IPv6 addresses from 2620:0:2d0:200:0:0:0:0 to 2620:0:2d0:200:ffff:ffff:ffff:ffff, type **2620:0:2d0:200::/64**.

      AWS WAF supports IPv4 address ranges: /8 and any range between /16 through /32. AWS WAF supports IPv6 address ranges: /16, /24, /32, /48, /56, /64, and /128. For more information about CIDR notation, see the Wikipedia entry Classless Inter-Domain Routing.

   3. To add more IP addresses, choose **Add another IP address** and type the value.

   4. Choose **Add**.

5. To delete an IP address or range:

   1. In the right pane, select the values that you want to delete.

   2. Choose **Delete IP address or range**.

## Deleting IP Match Conditions

If you want to delete an IP match condition, you must first delete all IP addresses and ranges in the condition and remove the condition from all the rules that are using it, as described in the following procedure.

**To delete an IP match condition**

1. Sign in to the AWS Management Console and open the AWS WAF console at https://console.aws.amazon.com/waf/.

2. In the navigation pane, choose **IP addresses**.

3. In the **IP match conditions** pane, choose the IP match condition that you want to delete.

4. In the right pane, choose the **Rules** tab.

   If the list of rules using this IP match condition is empty, go to step 6. If the list contains any rules, make note of the rules, and continue with step 5.

5. To remove the IP match condition from the rules that are using it, perform the following steps:

   1. In the navigation pane, choose **Rules**.

   2. Choose the name of a rule that is using the IP match condition that you want to delete.

   3. In the right pane, select the IP match condition that you want to remove from the rule, and choose **Remove selected condition**.

   4. Repeat steps b and c for all the remaining rules that are using the IP match condition that you want to delete.

5. In the navigation pane, choose **IP match conditions**.

6. In the **IP match conditions** pane, choose the IP match condition that you want to delete.

6. Choose **Delete** to delete the selected condition.

# Working with Geographic Match Conditions

If you want to allow or block web requests based on the country that the requests originate from, create one or more geo match conditions. A geo match condition lists countries that your requests originate from. Later in the process, when you create a web ACL, you specify whether to allow or block requests from those countries.

You can use geo match conditions with other AWS WAF conditions or rules to build sophisticated filtering. For example, if you want to block certain countries, but still allow specific IP addresses from that country, you could create a rule containing a geo match condition and an IP match condition. Configure the rule to block requests that originate from that country and do not match the approved IP addresses. As another example, if you want to prioritize resources for users in a particular country, you could include a geo match condition in two different rate-based rules. Set a higher rate limit for users in the preferred country and set a lower rate limit for all other users.

**Note**

If you are using the CloudFront geo restriction feature to block a country from accessing your content, any request from that country is blocked and is not forwarded to AWS WAF. So if you want to allow or block requests based on geography plus other AWS WAF conditions, you should *not* use the CloudFront geo restriction feature. Instead, you should use an AWS WAF geo match condition.

**Topics**

- Creating a Geo Match Condition
- Editing Geo Match Conditions
- Deleting Geo Match Conditions

## Creating a Geo Match Condition

If you want to allow some web requests and block others based on the countries that the requests originate from, create a geo match condition for the countries that you want to allow and another geo match condition for the countries that you want to block.

**Note**

When you add a geo match condition to a rule, you also can configure AWS WAF to allow or block web requests that *do not* originate from the country that you specify in the condition.

**To create a geo match condition**

1. Sign in to the AWS Management Console and open the AWS WAF console at https://console.aws.amazon.com/waf/.

2. In the navigation pane, choose **Geo match**.

3. Choose **Create condition**.

4. Type a name in the **Name** field.

   The name can contain only alphanumeric characters (A-Z, a-z, 0-9) or the following special characters: _-!"#'+*},./ . You can't change the name of a condition after you create it.

5. Choose a **Region**.

6. Choose a **Location type** and a country. **Location type** is currently limited to **Country**.

7. Choose **Add location**.

8. Choose **Create**.

76

## Editing Geo Match Conditions

You can add countries to or delete countries from your geo match condition.

**To edit a geo match condition**

1. Sign in to the AWS Management Console and open the AWS WAF console at https://console.aws.amazon.com/waf/.

2. In the navigation pane, choose **Geo match**.

3. In the **Geo match conditions** pane, choose the geo match condition that you want to edit.

4. To add a country:

   1. In the right pane, choose **Add filter**.

   2. Choose a **Location type** and a country. **Location type** is currently limited to **Country**.

   3. Choose **Add**.

5. To delete a country:

   1. In the right pane, select the values that you want to delete.

   2. Choose **Delete filter**.

## Deleting Geo Match Conditions

If you want to delete a geo match condition, you must first remove all countries in the condition and remove the condition from all the rules that are using it, as described in the following procedure.

**To delete a geo match condition**

1. Sign in to the AWS Management Console and open the AWS WAF console at https://console.aws.amazon.com/waf/.

2. Remove the geo match condition from the rules that are using it:

   1. In the navigation pane, choose **Rules**.

   2. Choose the name of a rule that is using the geo match condition that you want to delete.

   3. In the right pane, choose **Edit rule**.

   4. Choose the **X** next to the condition you want to delete.

   5. Choose **Update**.

   6. Repeat for all the remaining rules that are using the geo match condition that you want to delete.

3. Remove the filters from the condition you want to delete:

   1. In the navigation pane, choose **Geo match**.

   2. Choose the name of the geo match condition that you want to delete.

   3. In the right pane, choose the check box next to **Filter** in order to select all of the filters.

   4. Choose the **Delete filter**.

4. In the navigation pane, choose **Geo match**.

5. In the **Geo match conditions** pane, choose the geo match condition that you want to delete.

6. Choose **Delete** to delete the selected condition.

# Working with Size Constraint Conditions

If you want to allow or block web requests based on the length of specified parts of requests, create one or more size constraint conditions. A size constraint condition identifies the part of web requests that you want AWS WAF to look at, the number of bytes that you want AWS WAF to look for, and an operator, such as greater than (>) or less than (<). For example, you can use a size constraint condition to look for query strings that are longer than 100 bytes. Later in the process, when you create a web ACL, you specify whether to allow or block requests based on those settings.

Note that if you configure AWS WAF to inspect the request body, for example, by searching the body for a specified string, AWS WAF inspects only the first 8192 bytes (8 KB). If the request body for your web requests will never exceed 8192 bytes, you can create a size constraint condition and block requests that have a request body greater than 8192 bytes.

### Topics

- Creating Size Constraint Conditions
- Values That You Specify When You Create or Edit Size Constraint Conditions
- Adding and Deleting Filters in a Size Constraint Condition
- Deleting Size Constraint Conditions

## Creating Size Constraint Conditions

When you create size constraint conditions, you specify filters that identify the part of web requests for which you want AWS WAF to evaluate the length. You can add more than one filter to a size constraint condition, or you can create a separate condition for each filter. Here's how each configuration affects AWS WAF behavior:

- **One filter per size constraint condition** – When you add the separate size constraint conditions to a rule and add the rule to a web ACL, web requests must match all the conditions for AWS WAF to allow or block requests based on the conditions.

  For example, suppose you create two conditions. One matches web requests for which query strings are greater than 100 bytes. The other matches web requests for which the request body is greater than 1024 bytes. When you add both conditions to the same rule and add the rule to a web ACL, AWS WAF allows or blocks requests only when both conditions are true.

- **More than one filter per size constraint condition** – When you add a size constraint condition that contains multiple filters to a rule and add the rule to a web ACL, a web request needs only to match one of the filters in the size constraint condition for AWS WAF to allow or block the request based on that condition.

  Suppose you create one condition instead of two, and the one condition contains the same two filters as in the preceding example. AWS WAF allows or blocks requests if either the query string is greater than 100 bytes or the request body is greater than 1024 bytes.

### Note
When you add a size constraint condition to a rule, you also can configure AWS WAF to allow or block web requests that *do not* match the values in the condition.

### To create a size constraint condition

1. Sign in to the AWS Management Console and open the AWS WAF console at https://console.aws.amazon.com/waf/.

2. In the navigation pane, choose **Size constraints**.

3. Choose **Create condition**.

4. Specify the applicable filter settings. For more information, see Values That You Specify When You Create or Edit Size Constraint Conditions.

5. Choose **Add another filter.**

6. If you want to add another filter, repeat steps 4 and 5.

7. When you're finished adding filters, choose **Create size constraint condition**.

## Values That You Specify When You Create or Edit Size Constraint Conditions

When you create or update a size constraint condition, you specify the following values:

**Name**

Type a name for the size constraint condition.

The name can contain only alphanumeric characters (A-Z, a-z, 0-9) or the following special characters: _-!"#'+},./. You can't change the name of a condition after you create it.

**Part of the request to filter on**

Choose the part of each web request for which you want AWS WAF to evaluate the length:

**Header**

A specified request header, for example, the `User-Agent` or `Referer` header. If you choose **Header**, specify the name of the header in the **Header** field.

**HTTP method**

The HTTP method, which indicates the type of operation that the request is asking the origin to perform. CloudFront supports the following methods: `DELETE`, `GET`, `HEAD`, `OPTIONS`, `PATCH`, `POST`, and `PUT`.

**Query string**

The part of a URL that appears after a ? character, if any.

**URI**

The part of a URL that identifies a resource, for example, `/images/daily-ad.jpg`. Unless a **Transformation** is specified, a URI is not normalized and is inspected just as AWS receives it from the client as part of the request. A **Transformation** will reformat the URI as specified.

**Body**

The part of a request that contains any additional data that you want to send to your web server as the HTTP request body, such as data from a form.

**Single query parameter (value only)**

Any parameter that you have defined as part of the query string. For example, if the URL is "www.xyz.com?User-Name=abc&SalesRegion=seattle" you can add a filter to either the *UserName* or *SalesRegion* parameter.

If you choose **Single query parameter (value only)**, you will also specify a **Query parameter name**. This is the parameter in the query string that you will inspect, such as *UserName*. The maximum length for **Query parameter name** is 30 characters. **Query parameter name** is not case sensitive. For example, it you specify *UserName* as the **Query parameter name**, this will match all variations of *UserName*, such as *username* and *UsERName*.

**All query parameters (values only)**

Similar to **Single query parameter (value only)**, but rather than inspecting the value of a single parameter, AWS WAF inspects the values of all parameters within the query string for the size constraint. For example, if the URL is "www.xyz.com?UserName=abc&SalesRegion=seattle," and you choose **All query parameters (values only)**, AWS WAF will trigger a match the value of if either *UserName* or *SalesRegion* exceed the specified size.

**Header (Only When "Part of the request to filter on" is "Header")**

If you chose **Header** for **Part of the request to filter on**, choose a header from the list of common headers, or type the name of a header for which you want AWS WAF to evaluate the length.

**Comparison operator**

Choose how you want AWS WAF to evaluate the length of the query string in web requests with respect to the value that you specify for **Size**.

For example, if you choose **Is greater than** for **Comparison operator** and type **100** for **Size**, AWS WAF evaluates web requests for a query string that is longer than 100 bytes.

**Size**

Type the length, in bytes, that you want AWS WAF to watch for in query strings.

If you choose **URI** for the value of **Part of the request to filter on**, the / in the URI counts as one character. For example, the URI /logo.jpg is nine characters long.

**Transformation**

A transformation reformats a web request before AWS WAF evaluates the length of the specified part of the request. This eliminates some of the unusual formatting that attackers use in web requests in an effort to bypass AWS WAF.

If you choose **Body** for **Part of the request to filter on**, you can't configure AWS WAF to perform a transformation because only the first 8192 bytes are forwarded for inspection. However, you can still filter your traffic based on the size of the HTTP request body and specify a transformation of **None**. (AWS WAF gets the length of the body from the request headers.) You can only specify a single type of text transformation.

Transformations can perform the following operations:

**None**

AWS WAF doesn't perform any text transformations on the web request before checking the length.

**Convert to lowercase**

AWS WAF converts uppercase letters (A-Z) to lowercase (a-z).

**HTML decode**

AWS WAF replaces HTML-encoded characters with unencoded characters:

- Replaces &quot; with &
- Replaces   with a non-breaking space
- Replaces &lt; with <
- Replaces &gt; with >
- Replaces characters that are represented in hexadecimal format, &#xhhhh;, with the corresponding characters
- Replaces characters that are represented in decimal format, &#nnnn;, with the corresponding characters
  **Normalize whitespace**
  AWS WAF replaces the following characters with a space character (decimal 32):
- \f, formfeed, decimal 12
- \t, tab, decimal 9
- \n, newline, decimal 10
- \r, carriage return, decimal 13
- \v, vertical tab, decimal 11
- non-breaking space, decimal 160 In addition, this option replaces multiple spaces with one space.
  **Simplify command line**
  For requests that contain operating system command line commands, use this option to perform the following transformations:
- Delete the following characters: \ " ' ^
- Delete spaces before the following characters: / (
- Replace the following characters with a space: , ;
- Replace multiple spaces with one space
- Convert uppercase letters (A-Z) to lowercase (a-z)
  **URL decode**
  Decode a URL-encoded request.

## Adding and Deleting Filters in a Size Constraint Condition

You can add or delete filters in a size constraint condition. To change a filter, add a new one and delete the old one.

**To add or delete filters in a size constraint condition**

1. Sign in to the AWS Management Console and open the AWS WAF console at https://console.aws.amazon.com/waf/.

2. In the navigation pane, choose **Size constraint**.

3. Choose the condition that you want to add or delete filters in.

4. To add filters, perform the following steps:

   1. Choose **Add filter**.

   2. Specify the applicable filter settings. For more information, see Values That You Specify When You Create or Edit Size Constraint Conditions.

   3. Choose **Add**.

5. To delete filters, perform the following steps:

   1. Select the filter that you want to delete.

   2. Choose **Delete filter**.

## Deleting Size Constraint Conditions

If you want to delete a size constraint condition, you need to first delete all filters in the condition and remove the condition from all the rules that are using it, as described in the following procedure.

**To delete a size constraint condition**

1. Sign in to the AWS Management Console and open the AWS WAF console at https://console.aws.amazon.com/waf/.

2. In the navigation pane, choose **Size constraints**.

3. In the **Size constraint conditions** pane, choose the size constraint condition that you want to delete.

4. In the right pane, choose the **Associated rules** tab.

   If the list of rules using this size constraint condition is empty, go to step 6. If the list contains any rules, make note of the rules, and continue with step 5.

5. To remove the size constraint condition from the rules that are using it, perform the following steps:

   1. In the navigation pane, choose **Rules**.

   2. Choose the name of a rule that is using the size constraint condition that you want to delete.

   3. In the right pane, select the size constraint condition that you want to remove from the rule, and then choose **Remove selected condition**.

   4. Repeat steps b and c for all the remaining rules that are using the size constraint condition that you want to delete.

   5. In the navigation pane, choose **Size constraint**.

   6. In the **Size constraint conditions** pane, choose the size constraint condition that you want to delete.

6. Choose **Delete** to delete the selected condition.

# Working with SQL Injection Match Conditions

Attackers sometimes insert malicious SQL code into web requests in an effort to extract data from your database. To allow or block web requests that appear to contain malicious SQL code, create one or more SQL injection match conditions. A SQL injection match condition identifies the part of web requests, such as the URI or the query string, that you want AWS WAF to inspect. Later in the process, when you create a web ACL, you specify whether to allow or block requests that appear to contain malicious SQL code.

**Topics**

- Creating SQL Injection Match Conditions
- Values That You Specify When You Create or Edit SQL Injection Match Conditions
- Adding and Deleting Filters in a SQL Injection Match Condition
- Deleting SQL Injection Match Conditions

## Creating SQL Injection Match Conditions

When you create SQL injection match conditions, you specify filters, which indicate the part of web requests that you want AWS WAF to inspect for malicious SQL code, such as the URI or the query string. You can add more than one filter to a SQL injection match condition, or you can create a separate condition for each filter. Here's how each configuration affects AWS WAF behavior:

- **More than one filter per SQL injection match condition (recommended)** – When you add a SQL injection match condition containing multiple filters to a rule and add the rule to a web ACL, a web request needs only to match one of the filters in the SQL injection match condition for AWS WAF to allow or block the request based on that condition.

  For example, suppose you create one SQL injection match condition, and the condition contains two filters. One filter instructs AWS WAF to inspect the URI for malicious SQL code, and the other instructs AWS WAF to inspect the query string. AWS WAF allows or blocks requests if they appear to contain malicious SQL code *either* in the URI *or* in the query string.

- **One filter per SQL injection match condition** – When you add the separate SQL injection match conditions to a rule and add the rule to a web ACL, web requests must match all the conditions for AWS WAF to allow or block requests based on the conditions.

  Suppose you create two conditions, and each condition contains one of the two filters in the preceding example. When you add both conditions to the same rule and add the rule to a web ACL, AWS WAF allows or blocks requests only when both the URI and the query string appear to contain malicious SQL code.

**Note**
When you add a SQL injection match condition to a rule, you also can configure AWS WAF to allow or block web requests that *do not* appear to contain malicious SQL code.

**To create a SQL injection match condition**

1. Sign in to the AWS Management Console and open the AWS WAF console at https://console.aws.amazon.com/waf/.

2. In the navigation pane, choose **SQL injection**.

3. Choose **Create condition**.

4. Specify the applicable filter settings. For more information, see Values That You Specify When You Create or Edit SQL Injection Match Conditions.

5. Choose **Add another filter**.

6. If you want to add another filter, repeat steps 4 and 5.

7. When you're finished adding filters, choose **Create**.

## Values That You Specify When You Create or Edit SQL Injection Match Conditions

When you create or update a SQL injection match condition, you specify the following values:

**Name**

The name of the SQL injection match condition.

The name can contain only alphanumeric characters (A-Z, a-z, 0-9) or the following special characters: _-!"#'+*},./. You can't change the name of a condition after you create it.

**Part of the request to filter on**

Choose the part of each web request that you want AWS WAF to inspect for malicious SQL code:

**Header**

A specified request header, for example, the `User-Agent` or `Referer` header. If you choose **Header**, specify the name of the header in the **Header** field.

**HTTP method**

The HTTP method, which indicates the type of operation that the request is asking the origin to perform. CloudFront supports the following methods: `DELETE`, `GET`, `HEAD`, `OPTIONS`, `PATCH`, `POST`, and `PUT`.

**Query string**

The part of a URL that appears after a `?` character, if any.

**URI**

The part of a URL that identifies a resource, for example, `/images/daily-ad.jpg`. Unless a **Transformation** is specified, a URI is not normalized and is inspected just as AWS receives it from the client as part of the request. A **Transformation** will reformat the URI as specified.

**Body**

The part of a request that contains any additional data that you want to send to your web server as the HTTP request body, such as data from a form.

If you choose **Body** for the value of **Part of the request to filter on**, AWS WAF inspects only the first 8192 bytes (8 KB). To allow or block requests for which the body is longer than 8192 bytes, you can create a size constraint condition. (AWS WAF gets the length of the body from the request headers.) For more information, see Working with Size Constraint Conditions.

**Single query parameter (value only)**

Any parameter that you have defined as part of the query string. For example, if the URL is "www.xyz.com?User-Name=abc&SalesRegion=seattle" you can add a filter to either the *UserName* or *SalesRegion* parameter.

If you choose **Single query parameter (value only)** you will also specify a **Query parameter name**. This is the parameter in the query string that you will inspect, such as *UserName* or *SalesRegion*. The maximum length for **Query parameter name** is 30 characters. **Query parameter name** is not case sensitive. For example, it you specify *UserName* as the **Query parameter name**, this will match all variations of *UserName*, such as *username* and *UsERName*.

**All query parameters (values only)**

Similar to **Single query parameter (value only)**, but rather than inspecting the value of a single parameter, AWS WAF inspects the value of all parameters within the query string for possible malicious SQL code. For example, if the URL is "www.xyz.com?UserName=abc&SalesRegion=seattle," and you choose **All query parameters (values only)**, AWS WAF will trigger a match if the value of either *UserName* or *SalesRegion* contain possible malicious SQL code.

**Header**

If you chose **Header** for **Part of the request to filter on**, choose a header from the list of common headers, or type the name of a header that you want AWS WAF to inspect for malicious SQL code.

**Transformation**

A transformation reformats a web request before AWS WAF inspects the request. This eliminates some of the unusual formatting that attackers use in web requests in an effort to bypass AWS WAF.

You can only specify a single type of text transformation.

Transformations can perform the following operations:

**None**

AWS WAF doesn't perform any text transformations on the web request before inspecting it for the string in **Value to match**.

**Convert to lowercase**

AWS WAF converts uppercase letters (A-Z) to lowercase (a-z).

**HTML decode**

AWS WAF replaces HTML-encoded characters with unencoded characters:

- Replaces `&quot;` with &
- Replaces ` ` with a non-breaking space
- Replaces `&lt;` with <
- Replaces `&gt;` with >
- Replaces characters that are represented in hexadecimal format, `&#xhhhh;`, with the corresponding characters
- Replaces characters that are represented in decimal format, `&#nnnn;`, with the corresponding characters

    **Normalize whitespace**

    AWS WAF replaces the following characters with a space character (decimal 32):

- \f, formfeed, decimal 12
- \t, tab, decimal 9
- \n, newline, decimal 10
- \r, carriage return, decimal 13
- \v, vertical tab, decimal 11
- non-breaking space, decimal 160 In addition, this option replaces multiple spaces with one space.

    **Simplify command line**

    For requests that contain operating system command line commands, use this option to perform the following transformations:

- Delete the following characters: \ " ' ^
- Delete spaces before the following characters: / (
- Replace the following characters with a space: , ;
- Replace multiple spaces with one space
- Convert uppercase letters (A-Z) to lowercase (a-z)

    **URL decode**

    Decode a URL-encoded request.

## Adding and Deleting Filters in a SQL Injection Match Condition

You can add or delete filters in a SQL injection match condition. To change a filter, add a new one and delete the old one.

### To add or delete filters in a SQL injection match condition

1. Sign in to the AWS Management Console and open the AWS WAF console at https://console.aws.amazon.com/waf/.

2. In the navigation pane, choose **SQL injection**.

3. Choose the condition that you want to add or delete filters in.

4. To add filters, perform the following steps:

    1. Choose **Add filter**.

    2. Specify the applicable filter settings. For more information, see Values That You Specify When You Create or Edit SQL Injection Match Conditions.

    3. Choose **Add**.

5. To delete filters, perform the following steps:

1. Select the filter that you want to delete.

2. Choose **Delete filter**.

## Deleting SQL Injection Match Conditions

If you want to delete a SQL injection match condition, you need to first delete all filters in the condition and remove the condition from all the rules that are using it, as described in the following procedure.

**To delete a SQL injection match condition**

1. Sign in to the AWS Management Console and open the AWS WAF console at https://console.aws.amazon.com/waf/.

2. In the navigation pane, choose **SQL injection**.

3. In the **SQL injection match conditions** pane, choose the SQL injection match condition that you want to delete.

4. In the right pane, choose the **Associated rules** tab.

   If the list of rules using this SQL injection match condition is empty, go to step 6. If the list contains any rules, make note of the rules, and continue with step 5.

5. To remove the SQL injection match condition from the rules that are using it, perform the following steps:

   1. In the navigation pane, choose **Rules**.

   2. Choose the name of a rule that is using the SQL injection match condition that you want to delete.

   3. In the right pane, select the SQL injection match condition that you want to remove from the rule, and choose **Remove selected condition**.

   4. Repeat steps b and c for all of the remaining rules that are using the SQL injection match condition that you want to delete.

   5. In the navigation pane, choose **SQL injection**.

   6. In the **SQL injection match conditions** pane, choose the SQL injection match condition that you want to delete.

6. Choose **Delete** to delete the selected condition.

# Working with String Match Conditions

If you want to allow or block web requests based on strings that appear in the requests, create one or more string match conditions. A string match condition identifies the string that you want to search for and the part of web requests, such as a specified header or the query string, that you want AWS WAF to inspect for the string. Later in the process, when you create a web ACL, you specify whether to allow or block requests that contain the string.

**Topics**

- Creating a String Match Condition
- Values That You Specify When You Create or Edit String Match Conditions
- Adding and Deleting Filters in a String Match Condition
- Deleting String Match Conditions

## Creating a String Match Condition

When you create string match conditions, you specify filters that identify the string that you want to search for and the part of web requests that you want AWS WAF to inspect for that string, such as the URI or the query string. You can add more than one filter to a string match condition, or you can create a separate string match condition for each filter. Here's how each configuration affects AWS WAF behavior:

- **One filter per string match condition** – When you add the separate string match conditions to a rule and add the rule to a web ACL, web requests must match all the conditions for AWS WAF to allow or block requests based on the conditions.

  For example, suppose you create two conditions. One matches web requests that contain the value BadBot in the User-Agent header. The other matches web requests that contain the value BadParameter in query strings. When you add both conditions to the same rule and add the rule to a web ACL, AWS WAF allows or blocks requests only when they contain both values.

- **More than one filter per string match condition** – When you add a string match condition that contains multiple filters to a rule and add the rule to a web ACL, a web request needs only to match one of the filters in the string match condition for AWS WAF to allow or block the request based on the one condition.

  Suppose you create one condition instead of two, and the one condition contains the same two filters as in the preceding example. AWS WAF allows or blocks requests if they contain *either* BadBot in the User-Agent header *or* BadParameter in the query string.

**Note**
When you add a string match condition to a rule, you also can configure AWS WAF to allow or block web requests that *do not* match the values in the condition.

**To create a string match condition**

1. Sign in to the AWS Management Console and open the AWS WAF console at https://console.aws.amazon.com/waf/.

2. In the navigation pane, choose **String and regex matching**.

3. Choose **Create condition**.

4. Specify the applicable filter settings. For more information, see Values That You Specify When You Create or Edit String Match Conditions.

5. Choose **Add filter**.

6. If you want to add another filter, repeat steps 4 and 5.

7. When you're finished adding filters, choose **Create**.

## Values That You Specify When You Create or Edit String Match Conditions

When you create or update a string match condition, you specify the following values:

**Name**
Type a name for the string match condition. The name can contain only alphanumeric characters (A-Z, a-z, 0-9) or the following special characters: _-!"#'+*},./. You can't change the name of a condition after you create it.

**Type**
Choose **String match**.

**Part of the request to filter on**
Choose the part of each web request that you want AWS WAF to inspect for the string that you specify in **Value to match**:

**Header**
A specified request header, for example, the `User-Agent` or `Referer` header. If you choose **Header**, specify the name of the header in the **Header** field.

**HTTP method**
The HTTP method, which indicates the type of operation that the request is asking the origin to perform. CloudFront supports the following methods: `DELETE`, `GET`, `HEAD`, `OPTIONS`, `PATCH`, `POST`, and `PUT`.

**Query string**
The part of a URL that appears after a ? character, if any.

**URI**
The part of a URL that identifies a resource, for example, `/images/daily-ad.jpg`. Unless a **Transformation** is specified, a URI is not normalized and is inspected just as AWS receives it from the client as part of the request. A **Transformation** will reformat the URI as specified.

**Body**
The part of a request that contains any additional data that you want to send to your web server as the HTTP request body, such as data from a form.
If you choose **Body** for the value of **Part of the request to filter on**, AWS WAF inspects only the first 8192 bytes (8 KB). To allow or block requests for which the body is longer than 8192 bytes, you can create a size constraint condition. (AWS WAF gets the length of the body from the request headers.) For more information, see Working with Size Constraint Conditions.

**Single query parameter (value only)**
Any parameter that you have defined as part of the query string. For example, if the URL is "www.xyz.com?User-Name=abc&SalesRegion=seattle" you can add a filter to either the *UserName* or *SalesRegion* parameter.
If duplicate parameters appear in the query string, the values are evaluated as an "OR." That is, either value will trigger a match. For example, in the URL "www.xyz.com?SalesRegion=boston&SalesRegion=seattle", either "boston" or "seattle" in **Value to match** will trigger a match.
If you choose **Single query parameter (value only)** you will also specify a **Query parameter name**. This is the parameter in the query string that you will inspect, such as *UserName* or *SalesRegion*. The maximum length for **Query parameter name** is 30 characters. **Query parameter name** is not case sensitive. For example, it you specify *UserName* as the **Query parameter name**, this will match all variations of *UserName*, such as *username* and *UsERName*.

**All query parameters (values only)**
Similar to **Single query parameter (value only)**, but rather than inspecting the value of a single parameter, AWS WAF inspects the value of all parameters within the query string for the **Value to match**. For example, if the URL is "www.xyz.com?UserName=abc&SalesRegion=seattle," and you choose **All query parameters (values only)**, AWS WAF will trigger a match if the value of either *UserName* or *SalesRegion* is specified as the **Value to match**.

**Header (Only When "Part of the request to filter on" is "Header")**
If you chose **Header** from the **Part of the request to filter on** list, choose a header from the list of common headers, or type the name of a header that you want AWS WAF to inspect.

## Match type

Within the part of the request that you want AWS WAF to inspect, choose where the string in **Value to match** must appear to match this filter:

**Contains**

The string appears anywhere in the specified part of the request.

**Contains word**

The specified part of the web request must include **Value to match**, and **Value to match** must contain only alphanumeric characters or underscore (A-Z, a-z, 0-9, or _). In addition, **Value to match** must be a word, which means one of the following:

- **Value to match** exactly matches the value of the specified part of the web request, such as the value of a header.
- **Value to match** is at the beginning of the specified part of the web request and is followed by a character other than an alphanumeric character or underscore (_), for example, `BadBot;`.
- **Value to match** is at the end of the specified part of the web request and is preceded by a character other than an alphanumeric character or underscore (_), for example, `;BadBot`.
- **Value to match** is in the middle of the specified part of the web request and is preceded and followed by characters other than alphanumeric characters or underscore (_), for example, `-BadBot;`.

   **Exactly matches**

   The string and the value of the specified part of the request are identical.

   **Starts with**

   The string appears at the beginning of the specified part of the request.

   **Ends with**

   The string appears at the end of the specified part of the request.

## Transformation

A transformation reformats a web request before AWS WAF inspects the request. This eliminates some of the unusual formatting that attackers use in web requests in an effort to bypass AWS WAF.

You can only specify a single type of text transformation.

Transformations can perform the following operations:

**None**

AWS WAF doesn't perform any text transformations on the web request before inspecting it for the string in **Value to match.**

**Convert to lowercase**

AWS WAF converts uppercase letters (A-Z) to lowercase (a-z).

**HTML decode**

AWS WAF replaces HTML-encoded characters with unencoded characters:

- Replaces `&quot;` with &
- Replaces ` ` with a non-breaking space
- Replaces `&lt;` with <
- Replaces `&gt;` with >
- Replaces characters that are represented in hexadecimal format, `&#xhhhh;`, with the corresponding characters
- Replaces characters that are represented in decimal format, `&#nnnn;`, with the corresponding characters

   **Normalize whitespace**

   AWS WAF replaces the following characters with a space character (decimal 32):

- \f, formfeed, decimal 12
- \t, tab, decimal 9
- \n, newline, decimal 10
- \r, carriage return, decimal 13
- \v, vertical tab, decimal 11
- non-breaking space, decimal 160 In addition, this option replaces multiple spaces with one space.

   **Simplify command line**

   When you're concerned that attackers are injecting an operating system command line command and using unusual formatting to disguise some or all of the command, use this option to perform the following transformations:

- Delete the following characters: \ " ' ^
- Delete spaces before the following characters: / (
- Replace the following characters with a space: , ;
- Replace multiple spaces with one space
- Convert uppercase letters (A-Z) to lowercase (a-z)
  **URL decode**
  Decode a URL-encoded request.

**Value is base64 encoded**

If the value in **Value to match** is base64-encoded, select this check box. Use base64-encoding to specify non-printable characters, such as tabs and linefeeds, that attackers include in their requests.

**Value to match**

Specify the value that you want AWS WAF to search for in web requests. The maximum length is 50 bytes. If you're base64-encoding the value, the 50-byte limit applies to the value before you encode it.

## Adding and Deleting Filters in a String Match Condition

You can add filters to a string match condition or delete filters. To change a filter, add a new one and delete the old one.

**To add or delete filters in a string match condition**

1. Sign in to the AWS Management Console and open the AWS WAF console at https://console.aws.amazon.com/waf/.

2. In the navigation pane, choose **String and regex matching**.

3. Choose the condition that you want to add or delete filters in.

4. To add filters, perform the following steps:

   1. Choose **Add filter**.

   2. Specify the applicable filter settings. For more information, see Values That You Specify When You Create or Edit String Match Conditions.

   3. Choose **Add**.

5. To delete filters, perform the following steps:

   1. Select the filter that you want to delete.

   2. Choose **Delete Filter**.

## Deleting String Match Conditions

If you want to delete a string match condition, you need to first delete all filters in the condition and remove the condition from all the rules that are using it, as described in the following procedure.

**To delete a string match condition**

1. Sign in to the AWS Management Console and open the AWS WAF console at https://console.aws.amazon.com/waf/.

2. Remove the string match condition from the rules that are using it:

   1. In the navigation pane, choose **Rules**.

   2. Choose the name of a rule that is using the string match condition that you want to delete.

3. In the right pane, choose **Edit rule**.

4. Choose the **X** next to the condition you want to delete.

5. Choose **Update**.

6. Repeat for all the remaining rules that are using the string match condition that you want to delete.

3. Remove the filters from the condition you want to delete:

   1. In the navigation pane, choose **String and regex matching**.

   2. Choose the name of the string match condition that you want to delete.

   3. In the right pane, choose the check box next to **Filter** in order to select all of the filters.

   4. Choose the **Delete filter**.

4. In the navigation pane, choose **String and regex matching**.

5. In the **String and regex match conditions** pane, choose the string match condition that you want to delete.

6. Choose **Delete** to delete the selected condition.

# Working with Regex Match Conditions

If you want to allow or block web requests based on strings that match a regular expression (regex) pattern that appear in the requests, create one or more regex match conditions. A regex match condition is a type of string match condition that identifies the pattern that you want to search for and the part of web requests, such as a specified header or the query string, that you want AWS WAF to inspect for the pattern. Later in the process, when you create a web ACL, you specify whether to allow or block requests that contain the pattern.

## Topics

- Creating a Regex Match Condition
- Values That You Specify When You Create or Edit RegEx Match Conditions
- Editing a Regex Match Condition

## Creating a Regex Match Condition

When you create regex match conditions, you specify pattern sets that identify the string (using a regular expression) that you want to search for. You then add those pattern sets to filters that specify the part of web requests that you want AWS WAF to inspect for that pattern set, such as the URI or the query string.

You can add multiple regular expressions to a single pattern set. If you do so, those expressions are combined with an *OR*. That is, a web request will match the pattern set if the appropriate part of the request matches any of the expressions listed.

When you add a regex match condition to a rule, you also can configure AWS WAF to allow or block web requests that *do not* match the values in the condition.

AWS WAF supports most standard Perl Compatible Regular Expressions (PCRE). However, the following are not supported:

- Backreferences and capturing subexpressions
- Arbitrary zero-width assertions
- Subroutine references and recursive patterns
- Conditional patterns
- Backtracking control verbs
- The \C single-byte directive
- The \R newline match directive
- The \K start of match reset directive
- Callouts and embedded code
- Atomic grouping and possessive quantifiers

**To create a regex match condition**

1. Sign in to the AWS Management Console and open the AWS WAF console at https://console.aws.amazon.com/waf/.

2. In the navigation pane, choose **String and regex matching**.

3. Choose **Create condition**.

4. Specify the applicable filter settings. For more information, see Values That You Specify When You Create or Edit RegEx Match Conditions.

5. Choose **Create pattern set and add filter** (if you created a new pattern set) or **Add filter** if you used an existing pattern set.

6. Choose **Create**.

## Values That You Specify When You Create or Edit RegEx Match Conditions

When you create or update a regex match condition, you specify the following values:

**Name**

Type a name for the regex match condition. The name can contain only alphanumeric characters (A-Z, a-z, 0-9) or the following special characters: _-!"#'+*},./. You can't change the name of a condition after you create it.

**Type**

Choose **Regex match**.

**Part of the request to filter on**

Choose the part of each web request that you want AWS WAF to inspect for the pattern that you specify in **Value to match**:

**Header**

A specified request header, for example, the `User-Agent` or `Referer` header. If you choose **Header**, specify the name of the header in the **Header** field.

**HTTP method**

The HTTP method, which indicates the type of operation that the request is asking the origin to perform. CloudFront supports the following methods: `DELETE`, `GET`, `HEAD`, `OPTIONS`, `PATCH`, `POST`, and `PUT`.

**Query string**

The part of a URL that appears after a ? character, if any.

**URI**

The part of a URL that identifies a resource, for example, `/images/daily-ad.jpg`. Unless a **Transformation** is specified, a URI is not normalized and is inspected just as AWS receives it from the client as part of the request. A **Transformation** will reformat the URI as specified.

**Body**

The part of a request that contains any additional data that you want to send to your web server as the HTTP request body, such as data from a form.

If you choose **Body** for the value of **Part of the request to filter on**, AWS WAF inspects only the first 8192 bytes (8 KB). To allow or block requests for which the body is longer than 8192 bytes, you can create a size constraint condition. (AWS WAF gets the length of the body from the request headers.) For more information, see Working with Size Constraint Conditions.

**Single query parameter (value only)**

Any parameter that you have defined as part of the query string. For example, if the URL is "www.xyz.com?UserName=abc&SalesRegion=seattle" you can add a filter to either the *UserName* or *SalesRegion* parameter.

If duplicate parameters appear in the query string, the values are evaluated as an "OR." That is, either value will trigger a match. For example, in the URL "www.xyz.com?SalesRegion=boston&SalesRegion=seattle", a pattern that matches either "boston" or "seattle" in **Value to match** will trigger a match.

If you choose **Single query parameter (value only)** you will also specify a **Query parameter name**. This is the parameter in the query string that you will inspect, such as *UserName* or *SalesRegion*. The maximum length for **Query parameter name** is 30 characters. **Query parameter name** is not case sensitive. For example, it you specify *UserName* as the **Query parameter name**, this will match all variations of *UserName*, such as *username* and *UsERName*.

**All query parameters (values only)**

Similar to **Single query parameter (value only)**, but rather than inspecting the value of a single parameter, AWS WAF inspects the value of all parameters within the query string for the pattern specified in the **Value to match**. For example, in the URL "www.xyz.com?UserName=abc&SalesRegion=seattle", a pattern in **Value to match** that matches either the value in *UserName* or *SalesRegion* will trigger a match.

**Header (Only When "Part of the request to filter on" is "Header")**

If you chose **Header** from the **Part of the request to filter on** list, choose a header from the list of common headers, or type the name of a header that you want AWS WAF to inspect.

**Transformation**

A transformation reformats a web request before AWS WAF inspects the request. This eliminates some of the unusual formatting that attackers use in web requests in an effort to bypass AWS WAF.

You can only specify a single type of text transformation.

Transformations can perform the following operations:

**None**

AWS WAF doesn't perform any text transformations on the web request before inspecting it for the string in **Value to match.**

**Convert to lowercase**

AWS WAF converts uppercase letters (A-Z) to lowercase (a-z).

**HTML decode**

AWS WAF replaces HTML-encoded characters with unencoded characters:

- Replaces `&quot;` with `&`
- Replaces ` ` with a non-breaking space
- Replaces `&lt;` with `<`
- Replaces `&gt;` with `>`
- Replaces characters that are represented in hexadecimal format, `&#xhhhh;`, with the corresponding characters
- Replaces characters that are represented in decimal format, `&#nnnn;`, with the corresponding characters

  **Normalize whitespace**

  AWS WAF replaces the following characters with a space character (decimal 32):

- \f, formfeed, decimal 12
- \t, tab, decimal 9
- \n, newline, decimal 10
- \r, carriage return, decimal 13
- \v, vertical tab, decimal 11
- non-breaking space, decimal 160 In addition, this option replaces multiple spaces with one space.

  **Simplify command line**

  When you're concerned that attackers are injecting an operating system command line command and using unusual formatting to disguise some or all of the command, use this option to perform the following transformations:

- Delete the following characters: \ " ' ^
- Delete spaces before the following characters: / (
- Replace the following characters with a space: , ;
- Replace multiple spaces with one space
- Convert uppercase letters (A-Z) to lowercase (a-z)

  **URL decode**

  Decode a URL-encoded request.

**Regex pattern to match to request**

You can choose an existing pattern set, or create a new one. If you create a new one specify the following:

New pattern set name

Type a name and then specify the regex pattern that you want AWS WAF to search for.

If you add multiple regular expressions to a pattern set, those expressions are combined with an *OR*. That is, a web request will match the pattern set if the appropriate part of the request matches any of the expressions listed.

The maximum length of **Value to match** is 70 characters. If you want to specify a base64-encoded value, the limit is 70 characters before encoding.

## Editing a Regex Match Condition

You can make the following changes to an existing regex match condition:

- Delete a pattern from an existing pattern set
- Add a pattern to an existing pattern set
- Delete a filter to an existing regeex match condition

- Add a filter to an existing regeex match condition (You can have only one filter in a regex match condition. Therefore, in order to add a filter, you must delete the existing filter first.)
- Delete an existing regeex match condition

**Note**

You cannot add or delete a pattern set from an existing filter. You must either edit the pattern set, or delete the filter and create a new filter with a new pattern set.

**To delete a pattern from an existing pattern set**

1. Sign in to the AWS Management Console and open the AWS WAF console at https://console.aws.amazon.com/waf/.

2. In the navigation pane, choose **String and regex matching**.

3. Choose **View regex pattern sets**.

4. Choose the name of the pattern set you want to edit.

5. Choose **Edit**.

6. Choose the **X** next to the pattern you want to delete.

7. Choose **Save**.

**To add a pattern to an existing pattern set**

1. Sign in to the AWS Management Console and open the AWS WAF console at https://console.aws.amazon.com/waf/.

2. In the navigation pane, choose **String and regex matching**.

3. Choose **View regex pattern sets**.

4. Choose the name of the pattern set to edit.

5. Choose **Edit**.

6. Type a new regex pattern.

7. Choose the **+** next to the new pattern.

8. Choose **Save**.

**To delete a filter from an existing regex match condition**

1. Sign in to the AWS Management Console and open the AWS WAF console at https://console.aws.amazon.com/waf/.

2. In the navigation pane, choose **String and regex matching**.

3. Choose the name of the condition with the filter you want to delete.

4. Choose the box next to the filter you want to delete.

5. Choose **Delete filter**.

**To delete a regex match condition**

1. Sign in to the AWS Management Console and open the AWS WAF console at https://console.aws.amazon.com/waf/.

2. Delete the filter from the regex condition. See To delete a filter from an existing regex match condition for instructions to do this.)

3. Remove the regex match condition from the rules that are using it:

   1. In the navigation pane, choose **Rules**.

2. Choose the name of a rule that is using the regex match condition that you want to delete.

3. In the right pane, choose **Edit rule**.

4. Choose the **X** next to the condition you want to delete.

5. Choose **Update**.

6. Repeat for all the remaining rules that are using the regex match condition that you want to delete.

4. In the navigation pane, choose **String and regex matching**.

5. Select the button next to the condition you want to delete.

6. Choose **Delete**.

**To add or change a filter to an existing regex match condition**

You can have only one filter in a regex match condition. If you want to add or change the filter, you must first delete the existing filter.

1. Sign in to the AWS Management Console and open the AWS WAF console at https://console.aws.amazon.com/waf/.

2. Delete the filter from the regex condition you want to change. See To delete a filter from an existing regex match condition for instructions to do this.)

3. In the navigation pane, choose **String and regex matching**.

4. Choose the name of the condition you want to change.

5. Choose **Add filter**.

6. Enter the appropriate values for the new filter and choose **Add**.

# Working with Rules

Rules let you precisely target the web requests that you want AWS WAF to allow or block by specifying the exact conditions that you want AWS WAF to watch for. For example, AWS WAF can watch for the IP addresses that requests originate from, the strings that the requests contain and where the strings appear, and whether the requests appear to contain malicious SQL code.

**Topics**

- Creating a Rule and Adding Conditions
- Adding and Removing Conditions in a Rule
- Deleting a Rule
- AWS Marketplace Rule Groups

# Creating a Rule and Adding Conditions

If you add more than one condition to a rule, a web request must match all the conditions for AWS WAF to allow or block requests based on that rule.

**To create a rule and add conditions**

1. Sign in to the AWS Management Console and open the AWS WAF console at https://console.aws.amazon.com/waf/.

2. In the navigation pane, choose **Rules**.

3. Choose **Create rule**.

4. Type the following values:
   **Name**
   Type a name.
   **CloudWatch metric name**
   Type a name for the CloudWatch metric that AWS WAF will create and will associate with the rule. The name can contain only alphanumeric characters (A-Z, a-z, 0-9) or the following special characters: `_-!"#\+\*\},\./\.` It can't contain whitespace\. \*\*Rule type\*\* Choose eitherRegular ruleor Rate–based rule'. Rate–based rules are identical to regular rules, but also take into account how many requests arrive from a specified IP address every five minutes. For more information about these rule types, see How AWS WAF Works.
   **Rate limit**
   If you are creating a rate–based rule, enter the maximum number of requests from a single IP address allowed in a five-minute period. The rate limit must be equal to or greater than 2000.

5. To add a condition to the rule, specify the following values:
   **When a request does/does not**
   If you want AWS WAF to allow or block requests based on the filters in a condition, for example, web requests that originate from the range of IP addresses 192.0.2.0/24, choose **does**.
   If you want AWS WAF to allow or block requests based on the inverse of the filters in a condition, choose **does not**. For example, if an IP match condition includes the IP address range 192.0.2.0/24 and you want AWS WAF to allow or block requests that *do not* come from those IP addresses, choose **does not**.
   **match/originate from**
   Choose the type of condition that you want to add to the rule:

   - Cross-site scripting match conditions – choose **match at least one of the filters in the cross-site scripting match condition**
   - IP match conditions – choose **originate from an IP address in**
   - Geo match conditions – choose **originate from a geographic location in**
   - Size constraint conditions – choose **match at least one of the filters in the size constraint condition**
   - SQL injection match conditions – choose **match at least one of the filters in the SQL injection match condition**
   - String match conditions – choose **match at least one of the filters in the string match condition**
   - Regular expression match conditions – choose **match at least one of the filters in the regex match condition**
     **condition name**
     Choose the condition that you want to add to the rule. The list displays only conditions of the type that you chose in the preceding step.

6. To add another condition to the rule, choose **Add another condition**, and repeat steps 4 and 5. Note the following:

   - If you add more than one condition, a web request must match at least one filter in every condition for AWS WAF to allow or block requests based on that rule

- If you add two IP match conditions to the same rule, AWS WAF will only allow or block requests that originate from IP addresses that appear in both IP match conditions

7. When you're finished adding conditions, choose **Create**.

# Adding and Removing Conditions in a Rule

You can change a rule by adding or removing conditions.

**To add or remove conditions in a rule**

1. Sign in to the AWS Management Console and open the AWS WAF console at https://console.aws.amazon.com/waf/.

2. In the navigation pane, choose **Rules**.

3. Choose the name of the rule in which you want to add or remove conditions.

4. Choose **Add rule**.

5. To add a condition, choose **Add condition** and specify the following values:
   **When a request does/does not**
   If you want AWS WAF to allow or block requests based on the filters in a condition, for example, web requests that originate from the range of IP addresses 192.0.2.0/24, choose **does**.
   If you want AWS WAF to allow or block requests based on the inverse of the filters in a condition, choose **does not**. For example, if an IP match condition includes the IP address range 192.0.2.0/24 and you want AWS WAF to allow or block requests that *do not* come from those IP addresses, choose **does not**.
   **match/originate from**
   Choose the type of condition that you want to add to the rule:
   - Cross-site scripting match conditions – choose **match at least one of the filters in the cross-site scripting match condition**
   - IP match conditions – choose **originate from an IP address in**
   - Geo match conditions – choose **originate from a geographic location in**
   - Size constraint conditions – choose **match at least one of the filters in the size constraint condition**
   - SQL injection match conditions – choose **match at least one of the filters in the SQL injection match condition**
   - String match conditions – choose **match at least one of the filters in the string match condition**
   - Regular expression match conditions – choose **match at least one of the filters in the regex match condition**
     *condition name*
     Choose the condition that you want to add to the rule. The list displays only conditions of the type that you chose in the preceding step.

6. To remove a condition, select the **X** to the right of the condition name

7. Choose **Update**.

# Deleting a Rule

If you want to delete a rule, you need to first remove the rule from the web ACLs that are using it and remove the conditions that are included in the rule.

**To delete a rule**

1. Sign in to the AWS Management Console and open the AWS WAF console at https://console.aws.amazon.com/waf/.

2. To remove the rule from the web ACLs that are using it, perform the following steps:

    1. In the navigation pane, choose **Web ACLs**.

    2. Choose the name of a web ACL that is using the rule that you want to delete.

    3. Choose **Edit web ACL**.

    4. Choose the **X** to the right of the rule that you want to remove from the web ACL, and then choose **Update**.

    5. Repeat for all of the remaining web ACLs that are using the rule that you want to delete.

3. In the navigation pane, choose **Rules**.

4. Select the name of the rule you want to delete.

5. Choose **Delete**.

# AWS Marketplace Rule Groups

AWS WAF provides *AWS Marketplace rule groups* to help you protect your resources. AWS Marketplace rule groups are collections of predefined, ready-to-use rules that are written and updated by AWS and AWS partner companies.

Some AWS Marketplace rule groups are designed to help protect specific types of web applications like WordPress, Joomla, or PHP. Other AWS Marketplace rule groups offer broad protection against known threats or common web application vulnerabilities, such as those listed in the OWASP Top 10.

You can install a single AWS Marketplace rule group from your preferred AWS partner and also add your own customized AWS WAF rules for increased protection. If you are subject to regulatory compliance like PCI or HIPAA, you might be able to use AWS Marketplace rule groups to satisfy web application firewall requirements.

AWS Marketplace rule groups are available with no long-term contracts, and no minimum commitments. You are charged a monthly fee (pro-rated hourly) when subscribed to a rule group as well as ongoing request volume-based fees. For more information, see AWS WAF Pricing as well as the description for each AWS Marketplace rule group on AWS Marketplace.

## Automatic Updates

Keeping up to date on the constantly changing threat landscape can be time consuming and expensive. AWS Marketplace rule groups can save you time when you implement and use AWS WAF. Another benefit is that AWS and our AWS partners automatically update AWS Marketplace rule groups when new vulnerabilities and threats emerge.

Many of our partners are notified of new vulnerabilities before public disclosure. They can update their rule groups and deploy them to you even before a new threat is widely known. Many also have threat research teams to investigate and analyze the most recent threats in order to write the most relevant rules.

## Access to the Rules in an AWS Marketplace Rule Group

Each AWS Marketplace rule group provides a comprehensive description of the types of attacks and vulnerabilities that it's designed to protect against. To protect the intellectual property of the rule group providers, you can't view the individual rules within a rule group. This restriction also helps to keep malicious users from designing threats that specifically circumvent published rules.

Because you can't view individual rules in an AWS Marketplace rule group, you also can't edit any rules in a rule group. However, you can enable or disable entire rule groups, as well as choose the rule group action to perform. See Use AWS Marketplace Rule Groups for more information.

## Limits

You can enable only one AWS Marketplace rule group. This rule group counts towards the 10 rule limit per web ACL. Therefore you can have one AWS Marketplace rule group and up to nine custom rules in a single web ACL.

## Pricing

For AWS Marketplace rule group pricing, see AWS WAF Pricing as well as the description for each AWS Marketplace rule group on AWS Marketplace.

## Use AWS Marketplace Rule Groups

You can subscribe to and unsubscribe from AWS Marketplace rule groups on the AWS WAF console.

**To subscribe to and use an AWS Marketplace rule group**

1. Sign in to the AWS Management Console and open the AWS WAF console at https://console.aws.amazon. com/waf/.

2. In the navigation pane, choose **Marketplace**.

3. In the **Available marketplace products** section, choose the name of a rule group to view the details and pricing information.

4. If you want to subscribe to the rule group, choose **Continue**. **Note**
   If you don't want to subscribe to this rule group, simply close this page in your browser.

5. Choose **Set up your account**.

6. Add the rule group to a web ACL, just as you would add an individual rule. For more information, see Creating a Web ACL or Editing a Web ACL. **Note**
   When adding a rule group to a web ACL, the action you set for the rule group (either **No override** or **Override to count**) is called the rule group override action. For more information, see Rule Group Override.

**To unsubscribe from an AWS Marketplace rule group**

1. Sign in to the AWS Management Console and open the AWS WAF console at https://console.aws.amazon. com/waf/.

2. Remove the rule group from all web ACLs. For more information, see Editing a Web ACL.

3. In the navigation pane, choose **Marketplace**.

4. Choose **Manage your subscriptions**.

5. Choose **Cancel subscription** next to the name of the rule group that you want to unsubscribe from.

6. Choose **Yes, cancel subscription**.

## Rule Group Override

AWS Marketplace rule groups have two possible actions: **No override** and **Override to count**. If you want to test the rule group, set the action to **Override to count**. This rule group action will then override any *block* action specified by individual rules contained within the group. That is, if the rule group's action is set to **Override to count**, instead of potentially blocking matching requests based on the action of individual rules within the group, those requests will be counted. Conversely, if you set the rule group's action to **No override**, actions of the individual rules within the group will be used.

## Troubleshooting AWS Marketplace Rule Groups

If you find that an AWS Marketplace rule group is blocking legitimate traffic, perform the following steps.

**To troubleshoot an AWS Marketplace rule group**

1. Change the action for the AWS Marketplace rule group from **No override** to **Override to count**. This allows the web request to pass through, regardless of the individual rule actions within the rule group. This also provides you with Amazon CloudWatch metrics for the rule group.

2. After setting the AWS Marketplace rule group action to **Override to count**, contact the rule group provider's customer support team to further troubleshoot the issue. For contact information, see rule group listing on the product listing pages on AWS Marketplace.

**Contacting Customer Support**

For problems with AWS WAF or a rule group that is managed by AWS, contact AWS Support. For problems with a rule group that is managed by an AWS partner, contact that partner's customer support team. To find partner contact information, see the partner's listing on AWS Marketplace.

## Creating and Selling AWS Marketplace Rule Groups

If you want to sell AWS Marketplace rule groups on AWS Marketplace, see How to Sell Your Software on AWS Marketplace.

# Working with Web ACLs

When you add rules to a web ACL, you specify whether you want AWS WAF to allow or block requests based on the conditions in the rules. If you add more than one rule to a web ACL, AWS WAF evaluates each request against the rules in the order that you list them in the web ACL. When a web request matches all the conditions in a rule, AWS WAF immediately takes the corresponding action—allow or block—and doesn't evaluate the request against the remaining rules in the web ACL, if any.

If a web request doesn't match any of the rules in a web ACL, AWS WAF takes the default action that you specified for the web ACL. For more information, see Deciding on the Default Action for a Web ACL.

If you want to test a rule before you start using it to allow or block requests, you can configure AWS WAF to count the web requests that match the conditions in the rule. For more information, see Testing Web ACLs.

**Topics**

- Deciding on the Default Action for a Web ACL
- Creating a Web ACL
- Associating or Disassociating a Web ACL with a CloudFront Distribution or an Application Load Balancer
- Editing a Web ACL
- Deleting a Web ACL
- Testing Web ACLs

# Deciding on the Default Action for a Web ACL

When you create and configure a web ACL, the first and most important decision that you must make is whether the default action should be for AWS WAF to allow web requests or to block web requests. The default action indicates what you want AWS WAF to do after it inspects a web request for all the conditions that you specify, and the web request doesn't match any of those conditions:

- **Allow** – If you want to allow most users to access your website, but you want to block access to attackers whose requests originate from specified IP addresses, or whose requests appear to contain malicious SQL code or specified values, choose **Allow** for the default action.
- **Block** – If you want to prevent most would-be users from accessing your website, but you want to allow access to users whose requests originate from specified IP addresses, or whose requests contain specified values, choose **Block** for the default action.

Many decisions that you make after you've decided on a default action depend on whether you want to allow or block most web requests. For example, if you want to *allow* most requests, then the match conditions that you create generally should specify the web requests that you want to *block*, such as the following:

- Requests that originate from IP addresses that are making an unreasonable number of requests
- Requests that originate from countries that either you don't do business in or are the frequent source of attacks
- Requests that include fake values in the **User-Agent** header
- Requests that appear to include malicious SQL code

# Creating a Web ACL

**To create a web ACL**

1. Sign in to the AWS Management Console and open the AWS WAF console at https://console.aws.amazon. com/waf/.

2. If this is your first time using AWS WAF, choose **Go to AWS WAF** and then **Configure Web ACL**. If you've used AWS WAF before, choose **Web ACLs** in the navigation pane, and then choose **Create web ACL**.

3. For **Web ACL name**, type a name. **Note**
   You can't change the name after you create the web ACL.

4. For **CloudWatch metric name**, change the default name if applicable. The name can contain only alphanumeric characters (A-Z, a-z, 0-9) or the following special characters: _-!"#'+*},./. It can't contain whitespace. **Note**
   You can't change the name after you create the web ACL.

5. For **Region**, choose a region.

6. For **AWS resource**, choose the resource that you want to associate with this web ACL, and then choose **Next**.

7. If you've already created the conditions that you want AWS WAF to use to inspect your web requests, choose **Next**, and then continue to the next step.

   If you haven't already created conditions, do so now. For more information, see the following topics:
   - Working with Cross-site Scripting Match Conditions
   - Working with IP Match Conditions
   - Working with Geographic Match Conditions
   - Working with Size Constraint Conditions
   - Working with SQL Injection Match Conditions
   - Working with String Match Conditions
   - Working with Regex Match Conditions

8. If you've already created the rules (or subscribed to an AWS Marketplace rule group) that you want to add to this web ACL, add the rules to the web ACL:

   1. In the **Rules** list, choose a rule.

   2. Choose **Add rule to web ACL**.

   3. Repeat steps a and b until you've added all the rules that you want to add to this web ACL.

   4. Go to step 10.

9. If you haven't created rules yet, you can add rules now:

   1. Choose **Create rule**.

   2. Type the following values:
      **Name**
      Type a name.
      **CloudWatch metric name**
      Type a name for the CloudWatch metric that AWS WAF will create and will associate with the rule. The name can contain only alphanumeric characters (A-Z, a-z, 0-9). It can't contain whitespace. You can't change the metric name after you create the rule.

   3. To add a condition to the rule, specify the following values:
      **When a request does/does not**
      If you want AWS WAF to allow or block requests based on the filters in a condition, for example, web

106

requests that originate from the range of IP addresses 192.0.2.0/24, choose **does**.

If you want AWS WAF to allow or block requests based on the inverse of the filters in a condition, choose **does not**. For example, if an IP match condition includes the IP address range 192.0.2.0/24 and you want AWS WAF to allow or block requests that *do not* come from those IP addresses, choose **does not**.

match/originate from

Choose the type of condition that you want to add to the rule:

- Cross-site scripting match conditions – choose **match at least one of the filters in the cross-site scripting match condition**
- IP match conditions – choose **originate from an IP address in**
- Geo match conditions – choose **originate from a geographic location in**
- Size constraint conditions – choose **match at least one of the filters in the size constraint condition**
- SQL injection match conditions – choose **match at least one of the filters in the SQL injection match condition**
- String match conditions – choose **match at least one of the filters in the string match condition**
- Regex match conditions – choose **match at least one of the filters in the regex match condition**

    condition name

    Choose the condition that you want to add to the rule. The list displays only conditions of the type that you chose in the preceding list.

4. To add another condition to the rule, choose **Add another condition**, and then repeat steps b and c. Note the following:

   - If you add more than one condition, a web request must match at least one filter in every condition for AWS WAF to allow or block requests based on that rule
   - If you add two IP match conditions to the same rule, AWS WAF will only allow or block requests that originate from IP addresses that appear in both IP match conditions

5. Repeat step 9 until you've created all the rules that you want to add to this web ACL.

6. Choose **Create**.

7. Continue with step 10.

10. For each rule that you've added to the web ACL, choose whether you want AWS WAF to allow, block, or count web requests based on the conditions in the rule:

    - **Allow** – CloudFront or an Application Load Balancer responds with the requested object. In the case of CloudFront, if the object isn't in the edge cache, CloudFront forwards the request to the origin.

    - **Block** – CloudFront or an Application Load Balancer responds to the request with an HTTP 403 (Forbidden) status code. CloudFront also can respond with a custom error page. For more information, see Using AWS WAF with CloudFront Custom Error Pages.

    - **Count** – AWS WAF increments a counter of requests that match the conditions in the rule, and then continues to inspect the web request based on the remaining rules in the web ACL.

      For information about using **Count** to test a web ACL before you start to use it to allow or block web requests, see Counting the Web Requests That Match the Rules in a Web ACL. **Note**
      When adding an AWS Marketplace rule group to a web ACL (as opposed to a single rule), the action you set for the rule group (either **No override** or **Override to count**) is called the override action. For more information, see Rule Group Override.

11. If you want to change the order of the rules in the web ACL, use the arrows in the **Order** column. AWS WAF inspects web requests based on the order in which rules appear in the web ACL.

12. If you want to remove a rule that you added to the web ACL, choose the **x** in the row for the rule.

13. Choose the default action for the web ACL. This is the action that AWS WAF takes when a web request doesn't match the conditions in any of the rules in this web ACL. For more information, see Deciding on the Default Action for a Web ACL.

14. Choose **Review and create**.

15. Review the settings for the web ACL, and choose **Confirm and create**.

# Associating or Disassociating a Web ACL with a CloudFront Distribution or an Application Load Balancer

To associate or disassociate a web ACL, perform the applicable procedure. Note that you also can associate a web ACL with a CloudFront distribution when you create or update the distribution. For more information, see Using AWS WAF to Control Access to Your Content in the *Amazon CloudFront Developer Guide*.

The following restrictions apply when associating a web ACL:

- Web ACLs associated with an Application Load Balancer can only be associated with other Application Load Balancers in the same region.
- Web ACLs associated with a CloudFront distribution cannot be associated with an Application Load Balancer. The web ACL can, however, be associated with other CloudFront distributions.
- Each Application Load Balancer and CloudFront distribution can be associated with only one web ACL.

**To associate a web ACL with a CloudFront distribution or Application Load Balancer**

1. Sign in to the AWS Management Console and open the AWS WAF console at https://console.aws.amazon.com/waf/.

2. In the navigation pane, choose **Web ACLs**.

3. Choose the web ACL that you want to associate with a CloudFront distribution or Application Load Balancer.

4. On the **Rules** tab, under **AWS resources using this web ACL**, choose **Add association**.

5. When prompted, use the **Resource** list to choose the CloudFront distribution or Application Load Balancer that you want to associate this web ACL with. If you choose an Application Load Balancer, you also must specify a region.

6. Choose **Add**.

7. To associate this web ACL with additional CloudFront distributions or Application Load Balancers, repeat steps 4 through 6.

**To disassociate a web ACL from a CloudFront distribution or Application Load Balancer**

1. Sign in to the AWS Management Console and open the AWS WAF console at https://console.aws.amazon.com/waf/.

2. In the navigation pane, choose **Web ACLs**.

3. Choose the web ACL that you want to disassociate from a CloudFront distribution or Application Load Balancer.

4. On the **Rules** tab, under **AWS resources using this web ACL**, choose the **x** for each CloudFront distribution or Application Load Balancer that you want to disassociate this web ACL from.

# Editing a Web ACL

To add or remove rules from a web ACL or change the default action, perform the following procedure.

**To edit a web ACL**

1. Sign in to the AWS Management Console and open the AWS WAF console at https://console.aws.amazon.com/waf/.

2. In the navigation pane, choose **Web ACLs**.

3. Choose the web ACL that you want to edit.

4. On the **Rules** tab in the right pane, choose **Edit web ACL**.

5. To add rules to the web ACL, perform the following steps:

    1. In the **Rules** list, choose the rule that you want to add.

    2. Choose **Add rule to web ACL**.

    3. Repeat steps a and b until you've added all the rules that you want.

6. If you want to change the order of the rules in the web ACL, use the arrows in the **Order** column. AWS WAF inspects web requests based on the order in which rules appear in the web ACL.

7. To remove a rule from the web ACL, choose the **x** at the right of the row for that rule. This doesn't delete the rule from AWS WAF, it just removes the rule from this web ACL.

8. To change the action for a rule or the default action for the web ACL, choose the preferred option. **Note** When setting the action for an AWS Marketplace rule group (as opposed to a single rule), the action you set for the rule group (either **No override** or **Override to count**) is called the override action. For more information, see Rule Group Override

9. Choose **Save changes**.

# Deleting a Web ACL

To delete a web ACL, you must remove the rules that are included in the web ACL and disassociate all CloudFront distributions and Application Load Balancers from the web ACL. Perform the following procedure.

**To delete a web ACL**

1. Sign in to the AWS Management Console and open the AWS WAF console at https://console.aws.amazon.com/waf/.

2. In the navigation pane, choose **Web ACLs**.

3. Choose the web ACL that you want to delete.

4. On the **Rules** tab in the right pane, choose **Edit web ACL**.

5. To remove all rules from the web ACL, choose the **x** at the right of the row for each rule. This doesn't delete the rules from AWS WAF, it just removes the rules from this web ACL.

6. Choose **Update**.

7. Disassociate the web ACL from all CloudFront distributions and Application Load Balancers. On the **Rules** tab, under **AWS resources using this web ACL**, choose the **x** for each CloudFront distribution or Application Load Balancer.

8. On the **Web ACLs** page, confirm that the web ACL that you want to delete is selected, and then choose **Delete**.

# Testing Web ACLs

To ensure that you don't accidentally configure AWS WAF to block web requests that you want to allow or allow requests that you want to block, we recommend that you test your web ACL thoroughly before you start using it on your website or web application.

**Topics**

- Counting the Web Requests That Match the Rules in a Web ACL
- Viewing a Sample of the Web Requests That CloudFront or an Application Load Balancer Has Forwarded to AWS WAF

## Counting the Web Requests That Match the Rules in a Web ACL

When you add rules to a web ACL, you specify whether you want AWS WAF to allow, block, or count the web requests that match all the conditions in that rule. We recommend that you begin with the following configuration:

- Configure all the rules in a web ACL to count web requests
- Set the default action for the web ACL to allow requests

In this configuration, AWS WAF inspects each web request based on the conditions in the first rule. If the web request matches all the conditions in that rule, AWS WAF increments a counter for that rule. Then AWS WAF inspects the web request based on the conditions in the next rule. If the request matches all the conditions in that rule, AWS WAF increments a counter for the rule. This continues until AWS WAF has inspected the request based on the conditions in all of your rules.

After you've configured all the rules in a web ACL to count requests and associated the web ACL with a CloudFront distribution or Application Load Balancer, you can view the resulting counts in an Amazon CloudWatch graph. For each rule in a web ACL and for all the requests that CloudFront or an Application Load Balancer forwards to AWS WAF for a web ACL, CloudWatch lets you:

- View data for the preceding hour or preceding three hours,
- Change the interval between data points
- Change the calculation that CloudWatch performs on the data, such as maximum, minimum, average, or sum

**Note**
AWS WAF with CloudFront is a global service and metrics are available only when you choose the **US East (N. Virginia)** Region in the AWS console. If you choose another region, no AWS WAF metrics will appear in the CloudWatch console.

**To view data for the rules in a web ACL**

1. Sign in to the AWS Management Console and open the CloudWatch console at https://console.aws.amazon.com/cloudwatch/.

2. In the navigation pane, under **Metrics**, choose **WAF**.

3. Select the check box for the web ACL that you want to view data for.

4. Change the applicable settings:
   **Statistic**
   Choose the calculation that CloudWatch performs on the data.
   **Time range**
   Choose whether you want to view data for the preceding hour or the preceding three hours.
   **Period**
   Choose the interval between data points in the graph.

**Rules**

Choose the rules for which you want to view data.

Note the following:

- If you just associated a web ACL with a CloudFront distribution or Application Load Balancer, you might need to wait a few minutes for data to appear in the graph and for the metric for the web ACL to appear in the list of available metrics.
- If you associate more than one CloudFront distribution or Application Load Balancer with a web ACL, the CloudWatch data will include all the requests for all the distributions that are associated with the web ACL.
- You can hover the mouse cursor over a data point to get more information.
- The graph doesn't refresh itself automatically. To update the display, choose the refresh (↻) icon.

5. (Optional) View detailed information about individual requests that CloudFront or an Application Load Balancer has forwarded to AWS WAF. For more information, see Viewing a Sample of the Web Requests That CloudFront or an Application Load Balancer Has Forwarded to AWS WAF.

6. If you determine that a rule is intercepting requests that you don't want it to intercept, change the applicable settings. For more information, see Creating and Configuring a Web Access Control List (Web ACL).

When you're satisfied that all of your rules are intercepting only the correct requests, change the action for each of your rules to **Allow** or **Block**. For more information, see Editing a Web ACL.

## Viewing a Sample of the Web Requests That CloudFront or an Application Load Balancer Has Forwarded to AWS WAF

In the AWS WAF console, you can view a sample of the requests that CloudFront or an Application Load Balancer has forwarded to AWS WAF for inspection. For each sampled request, you can view detailed data about the request, such as the originating IP address and the headers included in the request. You also can view which rule the request matched, and whether the rule is configured to allow or block requests.

The sample of requests contains up to 100 requests that matched all the conditions in each rule and another 100 requests for the default action, which applies to requests that didn't match all the conditions in any rule. The requests in the sample come from all the CloudFront edge locations or Application Load Balancers that have received requests for your content in the previous 15 minutes.

**To view a sample of the web requests that CloudFront or an Application Load Balancer has forwarded to AWS WAF**

1. Sign in to the AWS Management Console and open the AWS WAF console at https://console.aws.amazon.com/waf/.

2. In the navigation pane, choose the web ACL for which you want to view requests.

3. In the right pane, choose the **Requests** tab.

   The **Sampled requests** table displays the following values for each request:
   **Source IP**
   Either the IP address that the request originated from or, if the viewer used an HTTP proxy or an Application Load Balancer to send the request, the IP address of the proxy or Application Load Balancer.
   **URI**
   The part of a URL that identifies a resource, for example, `/images/daily-ad.jpg`.
   **Matches rule**
   Identifies the first rule in the web ACL for which the web request matched all the conditions. If a web request doesn't match all the conditions in any rule in the web ACL, the value of **Matches rule** is **Default**.
   Note that when a web request matches all the conditions in a rule and the action for that rule is **Count**,

AWS WAF continues inspecting the web request based on subsequent rules in the web ACL. In this case, a web request could appear twice in the list of sampled requests: once for the rule that has an action of **Count** and again for a subsequent rule or for the default action.

**Action**

Indicates whether the action for the corresponding rule is **Allow**, **Block**, or **Count**.

**Time**

The time that AWS WAF received the request from CloudFront or your Application Load Balancer.

4. To display additional information about the request, choose the arrow on the left side of the IP address for that request. AWS WAF displays the following information:

**Source IP**

The same IP address as the value in the **Source IP** column in the table.

**Country**

The two-letter country code of the country that the request originated from. If the viewer used an HTTP proxy or an Application Load Balancer to send the request, this is the two-letter country code of the country that the HTTP proxy or an Application Load Balancer is in.

For a list of two-letter country codes and the corresponding country names, see the Wikipedia entry ISO 3166-1 alpha-2.

**Method**

The HTTP request method for the request: GET, HEAD, OPTIONS, PUT, POST, PATCH, or DELETE.

**URI**

The same URI as the value in the **URI** column in the table.

**Request headers**

The request headers and header values in the request.

5. To refresh the list of sample requests, choose **Get new samples**.

# Listing IP addresses blocked by rate-based rules

AWS WAF provides a list of IP addresses that are blocked by rate-based rules.

**To view addresses blocked by rate-based rules**

1. Sign in to the AWS Management Console and open the AWS WAF console at https://console.aws.amazon.com/waf/.

2. In the navigation pane, choose **Rules**.

3. In the **Name** column, choose a rate-based rule.

   The list shows the IP addresses that the rule currently blocks.

# How AWS WAF Works with Amazon CloudFront Features

When you create a web ACL, you can specify one or more CloudFront distributions that you want AWS WAF to inspect. AWS WAF starts to allow, block, or count web requests for those distributions based on the conditions that you identify in the web ACL. CloudFront provides some features that enhance the AWS WAF functionality. This chapter describes a few ways that you can configure CloudFront to make CloudFront and AWS WAF work better together.

**Topics**

- Using AWS WAF with CloudFront Custom Error Pages
- Using AWS WAF with CloudFront Geo Restriction
- Choosing the HTTP Methods That CloudFront Responds To

## Using AWS WAF with CloudFront Custom Error Pages

When AWS WAF blocks a web request based on the conditions that you specify, it returns HTTP status code 403 (Forbidden) to CloudFront. Next, CloudFront returns that status code to the viewer. The viewer then displays a brief and sparsely formatted default message similar to this:

`Forbidden: You don't have permission to access /myfilename.html on this server.`

If you'd rather display a custom error message, possibly using the same formatting as the rest of your website, you can configure CloudFront to return to the viewer an object (for example, an HTML file) that contains your custom error message.

**Note**
CloudFront can't distinguish between an HTTP status code 403 that is returned by your origin and one that is returned by AWS WAF when a request is blocked. This means that you can't return different custom error pages based on the different causes of an HTTP status code 403.

For more information about CloudFront custom error pages, see Customizing Error Responses in the *Amazon CloudFront Developer Guide*.

## Using AWS WAF with CloudFront Geo Restriction

You can use the Amazon CloudFront *geo restriction* feature, also known as *geoblocking*, to prevent users in specific geographic locations from accessing content that you distribute through a CloudFront web distribution. If you want to block web requests from specific countries and also block requests based on other conditions, you can use CloudFront geo restriction in conjunction with AWS WAF. CloudFront returns the same HTTP status code to viewers—HTTP 403 (Forbidden)—whether they try to access your content from a country on a CloudFront geo restriction blacklist or whether the request is blocked by AWS WAF.

**Note**
You can see the two-letter country code of the country that requests originate from in the sample of web requests for a web ACL. For more information, see Viewing a Sample of the Web Requests That CloudFront or an Application Load Balancer Has Forwarded to AWS WAF.

For more information about CloudFront geo restriction, see Restricting the Geographic Distribution of Your Content in the *Amazon CloudFront Developer Guide*.

## Choosing the HTTP Methods That CloudFront Responds To

When you create an Amazon CloudFront web distribution, you choose the HTTP methods that you want CloudFront to process and forward to your origin. You can choose from the following options:

- **GET, HEAD** – You can use CloudFront only to get objects from your origin or to get object headers.
- **GET, HEAD, OPTIONS** – You can use CloudFront only to get objects from your origin, get object headers, or retrieve a list of the options that your origin server supports.
- **GET, HEAD, OPTIONS, PUT, POST, PATCH, DELETE** – You can use CloudFront to get, add, update, and delete objects, and to get object headers. In addition, you can perform other POST operations such as submitting data from a web form.

You also can use AWS WAF string match conditions to allow or block requests based on the HTTP method, as described in Working with String Match Conditions. If you want to use a combination of methods that CloudFront supports, such as `GET` and `HEAD`, then you don't need to configure AWS WAF to block requests that use the other methods. If you want to allow a combination of methods that CloudFront doesn't support, such as `GET`, `HEAD`, and `POST`, you can configure CloudFront to respond to all methods, and then use AWS WAF to block requests that use other methods.

For more information about choosing the methods that CloudFront responds to, see Allowed HTTP Methods in the topic Values that You Specify When You Create or Update a Web Distribution in the *Amazon CloudFront Developer Guide*.

# Authentication and Access Control for AWS WAF

Access to AWS WAF requires credentials. Those credentials must have permissions to access AWS resources, such as an AWS WAF resource or an Amazon S3 bucket. The following sections provide details on how you can use AWS Identity and Access Management (IAM) and AWS WAF to help secure access to your resources.

- Authentication
- Access Control

## Authentication

You can access AWS as any of the following types of identities:

- **AWS account root user** – When you first create an AWS account, you begin with a single sign-in identity that has complete access to all AWS services and resources in the account. This identity is called the AWS account *root user* and is accessed by signing in with the email address and password that you used to create the account. We strongly recommend that you do not use the root user for your everyday tasks, even the administrative ones. Instead, adhere to the best practice of using the root user only to create your first IAM user. Then securely lock away the root user credentials and use them to perform only a few account and service management tasks.

- **IAM user** – An IAM user is an identity within your AWS account that has specific custom permissions (for example, permissions to create a rule in AWS WAF). You can use an IAM user name and password to sign in to secure AWS webpages like the AWS Management Console, AWS Discussion Forums, or the AWS Support Center.

  In addition to a user name and password, you can also generate access keys for each user. You can use these keys when you access AWS services programmatically, either through one of the several SDKs or by using the AWS Command Line Interface (CLI). The SDK and CLI tools use the access keys to cryptographically sign your request. If you don't use AWS tools, you must sign the request yourself. AWS WAF supports *Signature Version 4*, a protocol for authenticating inbound API requests. For more information about authenticating requests, see Signature Version 4 Signing Process in the *AWS General Reference*.

- **IAM role** – An IAM role is an IAM identity that you can create in your account that has specific permissions. It is similar to an *IAM user*, but it is not associated with a specific person. An IAM role enables you to obtain temporary access keys that can be used to access AWS services and resources. IAM roles with temporary credentials are useful in the following situations:

  - **Federated user access** – Instead of creating an IAM user, you can use existing user identities from AWS Directory Service, your enterprise user directory, or a web identity provider. These are known as *federated users*. AWS assigns a role to a federated user when access is requested through an identity provider. For more information about federated users, see Federated Users and Roles in the *IAM User Guide*.

  - **AWS service access** – You can use an IAM role in your account to grant an AWS service permissions to access your account's resources. For example, you can create a role that allows Amazon Redshift to access an Amazon S3 bucket on your behalf and then load data from that bucket into an Amazon Redshift cluster. For more information, see Creating a Role to Delegate Permissions to an AWS Service in the *IAM User Guide*.

118

- **Applications running on Amazon EC2** – You can use an IAM role to manage temporary credentials for applications that are running on an EC2 instance and making AWS API requests. This is preferable to storing access keys within the EC2 instance. To assign an AWS role to an EC2 instance and make it available to all of its applications, you create an instance profile that is attached to the instance. An instance profile contains the role and enables programs that are running on the EC2 instance to get temporary credentials. For more information, see Using an IAM Role to Grant Permissions to Applications Running on Amazon EC2 Instances in the *IAM User Guide*.

## Access Control

You can have valid credentials to authenticate your requests, but unless you have permissions you can't create or access AWS WAF resources. For example, you must have permissions to create an AWS WAF *web ACL* or *rule*.

The following sections describe how to manage permissions for AWS WAF. We recommend that you read the overview first.

- Overview of Managing Access Permissions to Your AWS WAF Resources
- Using Identity-Based Policies (IAM Policies) for AWS WAF
- AWS WAF API Permissions: Actions, Resources, and Conditions Reference

# AWS Identity and Access Management

AWS WAF integrates with AWS Identity and Access Management (IAM), a service that lets your organization do the following:

- Create users and groups under your organization's AWS account
- Share your AWS account resources with users in the account
- Assign unique security credentials to each user
- Control user access to services and resources

For example, you can use IAM with AWS WAF to control which users in your AWS account can create a new web ACL.

For general information about IAM, see the following documentation:

- AWS Identity and Access Management (IAM)
- IAM Getting Started Guide
- IAM User Guide

# Overview of Managing Access Permissions to Your AWS WAF Resources

Every AWS resource is owned by an AWS account, and permissions to create or access a resource are governed by permissions policies. An account administrator can attach permissions policies to IAM identities (that is, users, groups, and roles), and some services also support attaching permissions policies to resources.

**Note**

An *account administrator* (or administrator user) is a user with administrator privileges. For more information, see IAM Best Practices in the *IAM User Guide*.

When granting permissions, you decide who is getting the permissions, the resources they get permissions for, and the specific operations that you want to allow on those resources.

## Topics

- AWS WAF Resources and Operations
- Understanding Resource Ownership
- Managing Access to Resources
- Specifying Policy Elements: Actions, Effects, Resources, and Principals
- Specifying Conditions in a Policy

## AWS WAF Resources and Operations

In AWS WAF, the resources are *web ACLs* and *rules*. AWS WAF also supports conditions such as *byte match*, *IP match*, and *size constraint*.

These resources and conditions have unique Amazon Resource Names (ARNs) associated with them as shown in the following table.

| Name in WAF Console | Name in WAF SDK/CLI | ARN Format |
|---|---|---|
| Web ACL | WebACL | arn:aws:waf::*account:webacl/ID* |
| Rule | Rule | arn:aws:waf::*account:rule/ID* |
| String match condition | ByteMatchSet | arn:aws:waf::*account:bytematchset/ID* |
| SQL injection match condition | SqlInjectionMatchSet | arn:aws:waf::account:sqlinjectionset/ID |
| Size constraint condition | SizeConstraintSet | arn:aws:waf::account:sizeconstraintset/ID |
| IP match condition | IPSet | arn:aws:waf::account:ipset/ID |
| Cross-site scripting match condition | XssMatchSet | arn:aws:waf::account:xssmatchset/ID |

To allow or deny access to a subset of AWS WAF resources, include the ARN of the resource in the `resource` element of your policy. The ARNs for AWS WAF have the following format:

```
1  arn:aws:waf::account:resource/ID
```

Replace the *account*, *resource*, and *ID* variables with valid values. Valid values can be the following:

- *account*: The ID of your AWS account. You must specify a value.

- *resource*: The type of AWS WAF resource.
- *ID*: The ID of the AWS WAF resource, or a wildcard (∗) to indicate all resources of the specified type that are associated with the specified AWS account.

For example, the following ARN specifies all web ACLs for the account 111122223333:

```
1  arn:aws:waf::111122223333:webacl/*
```

For more information, see Resources in the *IAM User Guide*.

AWS WAF provides a set of operations to work with AWS WAF resources. For a list of available operations, see Actions.

## Understanding Resource Ownership

A *resource owner* is the AWS account that creates the resource. That is, the resource owner is the AWS account of the *principal entity* (the root account, an IAM user, or an IAM role) that authenticates the request that creates the resource. The following examples illustrate how this works:

- If you use the root account credentials of your AWS account to create an AWS WAF resource, your AWS account is the owner of the resource.
- If you create an IAM user in your AWS account and grant permissions to create an AWS WAF resource to that user, the user can create an AWS WAF resource. However, your AWS account, to which the user belongs, owns the AWS WAF resource.
- If you create an IAM role in your AWS account with permissions to create an AWS WAF resource, anyone who can assume the role can create an AWS WAF resource. Your AWS account, to which the role belongs, owns the AWS WAF resource.

## Managing Access to Resources

A *permissions policy* describes who has access to what. The following section explains the available options for creating permissions policies.

**Note**
This section discusses using IAM in the context of AWS WAF. It doesn't provide detailed information about the IAM service. For complete IAM documentation, see What Is IAM? in the *IAM User Guide*. For information about IAM policy syntax and descriptions, see AWS IAM Policy Reference in the *IAM User Guide*.

Policies that are attached to an IAM identity are known as *identity-based* policies and policies that are attached to a resource are known as *resource-based* policies. AWS WAF supports only identity-based policies.

**Topics**

- Identity-Based Policies (IAM Policies)
- Resource-Based Policies

**Identity-Based Policies (IAM Policies)**

You can attach policies to IAM identities. For example, you can do the following:

- **Attach a permissions policy to a user or a group in your account** – An account administrator can use a permissions policy that is associated with a particular user to grant permissions for that user to create an AWS WAF resource.

- **Attach a permissions policy to a role (grant cross-account permissions)** – You can attach an identity-based permissions policy to an IAM role to grant cross-account permissions. For example, the administrator in Account A can create a role to grant cross-account permissions to another AWS account (for example, Account B) or an AWS service as follows:

  1. Account A administrator creates an IAM role and attaches a permissions policy to the role that grants permissions on resources in Account A.

  2. Account A administrator attaches a trust policy to the role identifying Account B as the principal who can assume the role.

  3. Account B administrator can then delegate permissions to assume the role to any users in Account B. Doing this allows users in Account B to create or access resources in Account A. The principal in the trust policy also can be an AWS service principal if you want to grant an AWS service permissions to assume the role.

  For more information about using IAM to delegate permissions, see Access Management in the *IAM User Guide*.

The following is an example policy that grants permissions for the `waf:ListRules` action on all resources. In the current implementation, AWS WAF doesn't support identifying specific resources using the resource ARNs (also referred to as resource-level permissions) for some of the API actions, so you must specify a wildcard character (*):

```
1  {
2      "Version": "2012-10-17",
3      "Statement": [
4          {
5              "Sid": "ListRules",
6              "Effect": "Allow",
7              "Action": [
8                  "waf:ListRules"
9              ],
10             "Resource": "*"
11         }
12     ]
13 }
```

For more information about using identity-based policies with AWS WAF, see Using Identity-Based Policies (IAM Policies) for AWS WAF. For more information about users, groups, roles, and permissions, see Identities (Users, Groups, and Roles) in the *IAM User Guide*.

### Resource-Based Policies

Other services, such as Amazon S3, also support resource-based permissions policies. For example, you can attach a policy to an S3 bucket to manage access permissions to that bucket. AWS WAF doesn't support resource-based policies.

## Specifying Policy Elements: Actions, Effects, Resources, and Principals

For each AWS WAF resource (see AWS WAF Resources and Operations), the service defines a set of API operations (see AWS WAF API Permissions: Actions, Resources, and Conditions Reference). To grant permissions for these API operations, AWS WAF defines a set of actions that you can specify in a policy. Note that performing an API operation can require permissions for more than one action. When granting permissions for specific actions, you also identify the resource on which the actions are allowed or denied.

The following are the most basic policy elements:

- **Resource** – In a policy, you use an Amazon Resource Name (ARN) to identify the resource to which the policy applies. For more information, see AWS WAF Resources and Operations.
- **Action** – You use action keywords to identify resource operations that you want to allow or deny. For example, the `waf:CreateRule` permission allows the user permissions to perform the AWS WAF `CreateRule` operation.
- **Effect** – You specify the effect when the user requests the specific action. This can be either allow or deny. If you don't explicitly grant access to allow a resource, access is implicitly denied. You also can explicitly deny access to a resource, which you might do to make sure that a user cannot access it, even if a different policy grants access.
- **Principal** – In identity-based policies (IAM policies), the user that the policy is attached to is the implicit principal. AWS WAF doesn't support resource-based policies.

To learn more about IAM policy syntax and descriptions, see AWS IAM Policy Reference in the *IAM User Guide*.

For a table that shows all the AWS WAF API actions and the resources that they apply to, see AWS WAF API Permissions: Actions, Resources, and Conditions Reference.

## Specifying Conditions in a Policy

When you grant permissions, you can use the IAM policy language to specify the conditions when a policy should take effect. For example, you might want a policy to be applied only after a specific date. For more information about specifying conditions in a policy language, see Condition in the *IAM User Guide*.

To express conditions, you use predefined condition keys. There are no condition keys specific to AWS WAF. However, there are AWS-wide condition keys that you can use as appropriate. For a complete list of AWS-wide keys, see Available Keys for Conditions in the *IAM User Guide*.

# Using Identity-Based Policies (IAM Policies) for AWS WAF

This topic provides examples of identity-based policies that demonstrate how an account administrator can attach permissions policies to IAM identities (that is, users, groups, and roles) and thereby grant permissions to perform operations on AWS WAF resources.

**Important**

We recommend that you first review the introductory topics that explain the basic concepts and options available for you to manage access to your AWS WAF resources. For more information, see Overview of Managing Access Permissions to Your AWS WAF Resources.

The following shows an example of a permissions policy:

```
{
    "Version": "2012-10-17",
    "Statement": [
        {
            "Sid": "CreateFunctionPermissions",
            "Effect": "Allow",
            "Action": [
                "waf:ListWebACLs",
                "waf:ListRules",
                "waf:GetWebACL",
                "waf:GetRule",
                "cloudwatch:ListMetrics",
                "waf:GetSampledRequests"
            ],
            "Resource": "*"
        },
        {
            "Sid": "PermissionToPassAnyRole",
            "Effect": "Allow",
            "Action": [
                "iam:PassRole"
            ],
            "Resource": "arn:aws:iam::account-id:role/*"
        }
    ]
}
```

The policy has two statements:

- The first statement grants permissions to view statistics for AWS WAF web ACLs, using the `waf:ListWebACLs`, `waf:ListRules`, `waf:GetWebACL`, `waf:GetRule`, `cloudwatch:ListMetrics`, and `waf:GetSampledRequests` actions. AWS WAF doesn't support permissions for some of these actions at the resource level. Therefore, the policy specifies a wildcard character (*) as the `Resource` value.
- The second statement grants permissions for the IAM action `iam:PassRole` on IAM roles. The wildcard character (*) at the end of the `Resource` value means that the statement allows permissions for the `iam:PassRole` action on any IAM role. To limit these permissions to a specific role, replace the wildcard character (*) in the resource ARN with the specific role name.

The policy doesn't specify the `Principal` element because in an identity-based policy you don't specify the principal who gets the permissions. When you attach a policy to a user, the user is the implicit principal. When you attach a permissions policy to an IAM role, the principal identified in the role's trust policy gets the permissions.

For a table that shows all the AWS WAF API actions and the resources that they apply to, see AWS WAF API Permissions: Actions, Resources, and Conditions Reference.

## Topics

- Permissions Required to Use the AWS WAF Console
- AWS Managed (Predefined) Policies for AWS WAF
- Customer Managed Policy Examples

## Permissions Required to Use the AWS WAF Console

The AWS WAF console provides an integrated environment for you to create and manage AWS WAF resources. The console provides many features and workflows that often require permissions to create an AWS WAF resource in addition to the API-specific permissions that are documented in the AWS WAF API Permissions: Actions, Resources, and Conditions Reference. For more information about these additional console permissions, see Customer Managed Policy Examples.

## AWS Managed (Predefined) Policies for AWS WAF

AWS addresses many common use cases by providing standalone IAM policies that are created and administered by AWS. Managed policies grant necessary permissions for common use cases so you can avoid having to investigate what permissions are needed. For more information, see AWS Managed Policies in the *IAM User Guide*.

The following AWS managed policies, which you can attach to users in your account, are specific to AWS WAF and are grouped by use case scenario:

- **AWSWAFReadOnlyAccess** – Grants read-only access to AWS WAF resources.
- **AWSWAFFullAccess** – Grants full access to AWS WAF resources.

**Note**
You can review these permissions policies by signing in to the IAM console and searching for specific policies there.

You also can create your own custom IAM policies to allow permissions for AWS WAF API operations and resources. You can attach these custom policies to the IAM users or groups that require those permissions or to custom execution roles (IAM roles) that you create for your AWS WAF resources.

## Customer Managed Policy Examples

The examples in this section provide a group of sample policies that you can attach to a user. If you are new to creating policies, we recommend that you first create an IAM user in your account and attach the policies to the user, in the sequence outlined in the steps in this section.

You can use the console to verify the effects of each policy as you attach the policy to the user. Initially, the user doesn't have permissions, and the user won't be able to do anything in the console. As you attach policies to the user, you can verify that the user can perform various operations in the console.

We recommend that you use two browser windows: one to create the user and grant permissions, and the other to sign in to the AWS Management Console using the user's credentials and verify permissions as you grant them to the user.

For examples that show how to create an IAM role that you can use as an execution role for your AWS WAF resource, see Creating IAM Roles in the *IAM User Guide*.

## Example Topics

- Example 1: Give Users Read-only Access to AWS WAF, CloudFront, and CloudWatch
- Example 2: Give Users Full Access to AWS WAF, CloudFront, and CloudWatch
- Example 3: Granting Access to a Specified AWS Account
- Example 4: Granting Access to a Specified Web ACL

## Create an IAM User

First, you need to create an IAM user, add the user to an IAM group with administrative permissions, and then grant administrative permissions to the IAM user that you created. You then can access AWS using a special URL and the user's credentials.

For instructions, see Creating Your First IAM User and Administrators Group in the *IAM User Guide*.

## Example 1: Give Users Read-only Access to AWS WAF, CloudFront, and CloudWatch

The following policy grants users read-only access to AWS WAF resources, to Amazon CloudFront web distributions, and to Amazon CloudWatch metrics. It's useful for users who need permission to view the settings in AWS WAF conditions, rules, and web ACLs to see which distribution is associated with a web ACL, and to monitor metrics and a sample of requests in CloudWatch. These users can't create, update, or delete AWS WAF resources:

```
1  {
2      "Version":"2012-10-17",
3      "Statement": [
4          {
5              "Action": [
6                  "waf:Get*",
7                  "waf:List*",
8                  "cloudfront:GetDistribution",
9                  "cloudfront:GetDistributionConfig",
10                 "cloudfront:ListDistributions",
11                 "cloudfront:ListDistributionsByWebACLId",
12                 "cloudwatch:ListMetrics",
13                 "cloudwatch:GetMetricStatistics"
14             ],
15             "Effect": "Allow",
16             "Resource": "*"
17         }
18     ]
19 }
```

## Example 2: Give Users Full Access to AWS WAF, CloudFront, and CloudWatch

The following policy lets users perform any AWS WAF operation, perform any operation on CloudFront web distributions, and monitor metrics and a sample of requests in CloudWatch. It's useful for users who are AWS WAF administrators:

```
1  {
2      "Version": "2012-10-17",
3      "Statement": [
4          {
5              "Action": [
```

```
 6            "waf:*",
 7            "cloudfront:CreateDistribution",
 8            "cloudfront:GetDistribution",
 9            "cloudfront:GetDistributionConfig",
10            "cloudfront:UpdateDistribution",
11            "cloudfront:ListDistributions",
12            "cloudfront:ListDistributionsByWebACLId",
13            "cloudfront:DeleteDistribution",
14            "cloudwatch:ListMetrics",
15            "cloudwatch:GetMetricStatistics"
16          ],
17          "Effect": "Allow",
18          "Resource": "*"
19        }
20      ]
21  }
```

We strongly recommend that you configure multi-factor authentication (MFA) for users who have administrative permissions. For more information, see Using Multi-Factor Authentication (MFA) Devices with AWS in the *IAM User Guide*.

### Example 3: Granting Access to a Specified AWS Account

This policy grants the following permissions to the account 444455556666:

- Full access to all AWS WAF operations and resources.
- Read and update access to all CloudFront distributions, which allows you to associate web ACLs and CloudFront distributions.
- Read access to all CloudWatch metrics and metric statistics, so that you can view CloudWatch data and a sample of requests in the AWS WAF console.

```
 1  {
 2    "Version": "2012-10-17",
 3    "Statement": [
 4      {
 5        "Effect": "Allow",
 6        "Action": [
 7          "waf:*"
 8        ],
 9        "Resource": [
10          "arn:aws:waf::444455556666:*"
11        ]
12      },
13      {
14        "Effect": "Allow",
15        "Action": [
16          "cloudfront:GetDistribution",
17          "cloudfront:GetDistributionConfig",
18          "cloudfront:ListDistributions",
19          "cloudfront:ListDistributionsByWebACLId",
20          "cloudfront:UpdateDistributions",
21          "cloudwatch:ListMetrics",
22          "cloudwatch:GetMetricStatistics"
23        ],
24        "Resource": [
```

```
25            "*"
26         ]
27      }
28   ]
29 }
```

## Example 4: Granting Access to a Specified Web ACL

This policy grants the following permissions to the `webacl` ID 112233d7c-86b2-458b-af83-51c51example in the account 444455556666:

- Full access to AWS WAF `Get`, `Update`, and `Delete` operations and resources

```
1  {
2     "Version": "2012-10-17",
3     "Statement": [
4        {
5           "Effect": "Allow",
6           "Action": [
7              "waf:*"
8           ],
9           "Resource": [
10             "arn:aws:waf::444455556666:webacl/112233d7c-86b2-458b-af83-51c51example"
11          ]
12       }
13    ]
14 }
```

# AWS WAF API Permissions: Actions, Resources, and Conditions Reference

When you are setting up Access Control and writing permissions policies that you can attach to an IAM identity (identity-based policies), you can use the following table as a reference. The table lists each AWS WAF API operation, the corresponding actions for which you can grant permissions to perform the action, and the AWS resource for which you can grant the permissions. You specify the actions in the policy's `Action` field, and you specify the resource value in the policy's `Resource` field.

You can use AWS-wide condition keys in your AWS WAF policies to express conditions. For a complete list of AWS-wide keys, see Available Keys for Conditions in the *IAM User Guide*.

**Note**

To specify an action, use the `waf:` prefix followed by the API operation name (for example, `waf:CreateIPSet`).

# AWS WAF Limits

AWS WAF has default limits on the number of entities per account. You can request an increase in these limits.

| Resource | Default Limit |
| --- | --- |
| Web ACLs per AWS account | 50 |
| Rules per AWS account | 100 |
| Rate-based-rules per AWS account | 5 |
| Conditions per AWS account | 100 of each condition type (For example: 100 size constraint conditions, 100 IP match conditions, and so on. The exception is regex match conditions. You can have a maximum of 10 regex match conditions per account. This limit cannot be increased.) |
| Requests per Second | 10,000 per web ACL* |

*This limit applies only to AWS WAF on an Application Load Balancer. Requests per Second (RPS) limits for AWS WAF on CloudFront are the same as the RPS limits support by CloudFront that is described in the CloudFront Developer Guide.

The following limits on AWS WAF entities can't be changed.

| Resource | Limit |
| --- | --- |
| Rules per web ACL | 10 |
| Conditions per rule | 10 |
| IP address ranges (in CIDR notation) per IP match condition | 10,000 |
| IP addresses blocked per rate-based rule | 10,000 |
| Minimum rate-based rule rate limit per 5 minute period | 2000 |
| Filters per cross-site scripting match condition | 10 |
| Filters per size constraint condition | 10 |
| Filters per SQL injection match condition | 10 |
| Filters per string match condition | 10 |
| In string match conditions, the number of characters in HTTP header names, when you've configured AWS WAF to inspect the headers in web requests for a specified value | 40 |
| In string match conditions, the number of characters in the value that you want AWS WAF to search for | 50 |
| In regex match conditions, the number of characters in the pattern that you want AWS WAF to search for | 70 |
| In regex match conditions, the number of patterns per pattern set | 10 |
| In regex match conditions, the number of pattern sets per regex condition | 1 |
| The number of pattern sets per account | 5 |
| GeoMatchSets per account | 50 |
| Locations per GeoMatchSet | 50 |

# AWS Firewall Manager

AWS Firewall Manager simplifies your AWS WAF administration and maintenance tasks across multiple accounts and resources. With Firewall Manager, you set up your firewall rules just once. The service automatically applies your rules across your accounts and resources, even as you add new resources.

Firewall Manager provides these benefits:

- Helps to protect resources across accounts
- Helps to protect all resources of a particular type, such as all Amazon CloudFront distributions
- Helps to protect all resources with specific tags
- Automatically adds protection to resources that are added to your account
- Lets you use your own custom rules, or purchase managed rules from AWS Marketplace

Firewall Manager is particularly useful when you have a large number of resources that you want to protect with AWS WAF, or if you frequently add new resources that you want to protect.

To use Firewall Manager, you add rules to a rule group, and you add the rule group to a policy. Firewall Manager applies the policy to resource types that you specify (such as CloudFront distributions or Application Load Balancers) in all accounts within your organization in AWS Organizations. If you add a new account to your organization, Firewall Manager automatically applies the policy to the specified resources in that account.

**Topics**

- AWS Firewall Manager Pricing
- AWS Firewall Manager Prerequisites
- Getting Started with AWS Firewall Manager
- AWS Firewall Manager Limits
- Working with Rule Groups
- Working with AWS Firewall Manager Policies
- Viewing Resource Compliance with a Policy
- Designating a Different Account as the AWS Firewall Manager Administrator Account

# AWS Firewall Manager Pricing

AWS Firewall Manager incurs charges for AWS WAF web ACLs and rules that you create, along with charges for some related services. For more information, see AWS Firewall Manager Pricing.

# AWS Firewall Manager Prerequisites

This topic shows you how to prepare your account to use AWS Firewall Manager. Before you use Firewall Manager for the first time, perform all the following steps in sequence.

**Topics**

- Step 1: Join AWS Organizations
- Step 2: Set the AWS Firewall Manager Administrator Account
- Step 3: Enable AWS Config

# Step 1: Join AWS Organizations

To use AWS Firewall Manager, your account must be a member of an organization in the AWS Organizations service. If your account is already a member, you can skip this step and go to Step 2: Set the AWS Firewall Manager Administrator Account.

**Note**
AWS Organizations has two available feature sets: *consolidated billing features* and *all features*. To use Firewall Manager, the organization that you belong to must be enabled for all features. If your organization is configured only for consolidated billing, see Enabling All Features in Your Organization.

If your account is not part of an organization, create or join an organization as described in Creating and Managing an AWS Organizations.

After your account is a member of an organization, go to Step 2: Set the AWS Firewall Manager Administrator Account.

# Step 2: Set the AWS Firewall Manager Administrator Account

AWS Firewall Manager must be associated with the master account of your AWS organization or associated with a member account that has the appropriate permissions. The account that you associate with Firewall Manager is called the Firewall Manager administrator account.

For more information about AWS Organizations and master accounts, see Managing the AWS Accounts in Your Organization.

**To set the Firewall Manager administrator account (console)**

1. Sign in to the AWS Management Console using an existing AWS Organizations master account. You can sign in using the account's root user (not recommended) or another IAM user or IAM role within the account that has equivalent permissions.

2. Open the Firewall Manager console at https://console/.aws/.amazon/.com/waf/fms/.

3. Choose **Get started**.

4. Type an account ID to associate with Firewall Manager. This will be the Firewall Manager administrator account. The account ID can be the account that you are signed in with, or a different account. If the account ID that you type is not an AWS Organizations master account, Firewall Manager sets the appropriate permissions for the member account that you specify. **Note**
The account that you enter in this step is given permission to create and manage AWS WAF rules across all accounts within your organization.

5. Choose **Set administrator**.

After you set the AWS Firewall Manager administrator account, go to Step 3: Enable AWS Config.

# Step 3: Enable AWS Config

Enable AWS Config for each member account in your AWS organization. For more information, see Getting Started with AWS Config.

You must enable AWS Config for each AWS Region that contains the resources that you want to protect. You can enable AWS Config manually, or you can use the AWS CloudFormation template "Enable AWS Config" at AWS CloudFormation StackSets Sample Templates.

You must, at a minimum, specify the following resource types that you want to protect with AWS Firewall Manager: Application Load Balancers, CloudFront distributions, or both.

When enabling AWS Config to protect an Application Load Balancer, choose **ElasticLoadBalancingV2** in the provided list of resource types.

When enabling AWS Config to protect a CloudFront distribution, you must be in the US East (N. Virginia) region. Other regions will not have CloudFront as an option.

You can now configure AWS Firewall Manager to begin protecting your resources. For more information, see Getting Started with AWS Firewall Manager .

# Getting Started with AWS Firewall Manager

This topic shows you how to get started with AWS Firewall Manager. Perform the following steps in sequence.

**Topics**

- Step 1: Complete the Prerequisites
- Step 2: Create Rules
- Step 3: Create a Rule Group
- Step 4: Create and Apply an AWS Firewall Manager Policy

# Step 1: Complete the Prerequisites

There are several mandatory steps to prepare your account for AWS Firewall Manager. Those steps are described in AWS Firewall Manager Prerequisites. Complete all the prerequisites before proceeding to Step 2: Create Rules.

# Step 2: Create Rules

In this step, you create rules using AWS WAF. If you already have AWS WAF rules that you want to use with AWS Firewall Manager, skip this step and go to Step 3: Create a Rule Group.

**To create AWS WAF rules (console)**

1. Create your conditions. For more information, see Working with conditions.

2. Create your rules, and then add your conditions to your rules. For more information, see Creating a Rule and Adding Conditions.

You are now ready to go to Step 3: Create a Rule Group.

# Step 3: Create a Rule Group

A rule group is a set of rules that defines what actions to take when a particular set of conditions is met. You can purchase managed rule groups from AWS Marketplace, or you can create your own rule group.

To purchase a managed rule group from AWS Marketplace, see AWS Marketplace Rule Groups.

To create your own rule group, perform the following procedure.

**To create a rule group**

1. Sign in to the AWS Management Console using the AWS Firewall Manager administrator account that you set up in the prerequisites, and then open the Firewall Manager console at https://console/.aws/.amazon/ .com/waf/fms/.

2. In the navigation pane, choose **Security policies**.

3. If you have not met the prerequisites, the console displays instructions about how to fix any issues. Follow the instructions, and then begin this step (create a rule group) again. If you have met the prerequisites, choose **Close**.

4. Choose **Create policy**.

5. Choose **Create an AWS Firewall Manager policy and add a new rule group.**.

6. Choose an AWS Region, and then choose **Next**.

7. Because you already created rules, you don't need to create conditions. Choose **Next**.

8. Because you already created rules, you don't need to create rules. Choose **Next**.

9. Choose **Create rule group**.

10. For **Name**, type a friendly name.

11. Type a name for the CloudWatch metric that AWS WAF will create and will associate with the rule group. The name can contain only alphanumeric characters (A-Z, a-z, 0-9) or the following special characters: _-!"#'+*},./. It can't contain whitespace.

12. Select a rule, and then choose **Add rule**. Repeat adding rules until you have added all the rules that you want to the rule group.

13. A rule group has two possible actions: **Block** and **Count**. If you want to test the rule group, set the action to **Count**. This action overrides any *block* action specified by individual rules contained in the group. That is, if the rule group's action is set to **Count**, requests are only counted and not blocked. Conversely, if you set the rule group's action to **Block**, actions of the individual rules in the group are used. For this tutorial, choose **Count**.

14. Choose **Create**.

You are now ready to go to Step 4: Create and Apply an AWS Firewall Manager Policy

# Step 4: Create and Apply an AWS Firewall Manager Policy

After you create the rule group, you create an AWS Firewall Manager policy. A Firewall Manager policy contains the rule group that you want to apply to your resources.

**To create a Firewall Manager policy (console)**

1. After you create the rule group (the last step in the preceding procedure, Step 3: Create a Rule Group), the console displays the **Rule group summary** page. Choose **Next**.

2. For **Name**, type a friendly name.

3. For **Region**, choose an AWS Region.

4. Select a rule group to add, and then choose **Add rule group**.

5. A policy has two possible actions: **Action set by rule group** and **Count**. If you want to test the policy and rule group, set the action to **Count**. This action overrides any *block* action specified by the rule group contained in the policy. That is, if the policy's action is set to **Count**, those requests are only counted and not blocked. Conversely, if you set the policy's action to **Action set by rule group**, actions of the rule group in the policy are used. For this tutorial, choose **Count**.

6. Choose **Next**.

7. Choose the type of resource that you want to protect.

8. If you want to protect only resources with specific tags, or alternatively exclude resources with specific tags, select **Use tags to include/exclude resources**, type the tags and then choose either **Include** or **Exclude**. You can choose only one option.

   If you enter more than one tag (separated by commas), and if a resource has any of those tags, it is considered a match.

   For more information about tags, see Working with Tag Editor .

9. Choose **Create and apply this policy to existing and new resources**.

   This option creates a web ACL in each account within an organization in AWS Organizations, and associates the web ACL with the specified resources in the accounts. This option also applies the policy to all new resources that match the above criteria (resource type and tags). Alternatively, if you choose **Create policy but do not apply the policy to existing or new resources**, Firewall Manager creates a web ACL in each account within the organization, but doesn't apply the web ACL to any resources. You must apply the policy to resources later.

10. Choose **Next**.

11. Review the new policy. To make any changes, choose **Edit**. When you are satisfied with the policy, choose **Create policy. Note**
    Firewall Manager applies a policy to all accounts in your organization in AWS Organizations. You can't include or exclude individual accounts. If you add a new account to the organization, Firewall Manager automatically applies the policy to that account.

# AWS Firewall Manager Limits

AWS Firewall Manager has default limits on the number of entities per account. You can request an increase in these limits.

| Resource | Default Limit |
|---|---|
| Accounts per organization in AWS Organizations | Varies. An invitation sent to an account counts against this limit. The count is returned if the invited account declines, the master account cancels the invitation, or the invitation expires. |
| Firewall Manager policies per organization in AWS Organizations | 20 |
| Tags that include or exclude resources per Firewall Manager policy | 8 |

The following limits related to AWSFirewall Manager can't be changed.

| Resource | Limit |
|---|---|
| Rule groups per Firewall Manager administrator account | 3 |
| Rule groups per Firewall Manager policy | 1 |
| Rules per rule group | 10 |

# Working with Rule Groups

A *rule group* is a set of rules that you add to a web ACL or an AWS Firewall Manager policy. You can create your own rule group, or you can purchase a managed rule group from AWS Marketplace. For more information, see AWS Marketplace Rule Groups.

**Important**
If you want to add an AWS Marketplace rule group to your policy, each account in your organization must first subscribe to that rule group. After all accounts have subscribed, you can then add the rule group to a policy. For more information, see AWS Marketplace Rule Groups.

**Topics**

- Creating a Rule Group
- Adding and Deleting Rules from a Rule Group

# Creating a Rule Group

When you create a rule group to use with AWS Firewall Manager, you specify which rules to add to the group.

**To create a rule group (console)**

1. Sign in to the AWS Management Console using the AWS Firewall Manager administrator account that you set up in the prerequisites, and then open the Firewall Manager console at https://console/.aws/.amazon/ .com/waf/fms/. **Note**
For information about setting up a Firewall Manager administrator account, see Step 2: Set the AWS Firewall Manager Administrator Account.

2. In the navigation pane, choose **Rule groups**.

3. Choose **Create rule group**.

4. If you have already created the rules that you want to add to the rule group, choose **Use existing rules for this rule group **. If you want to create new rules to add to the rule group, choose **Create rules and conditions for this rule group**. **Note**
You cannot add rate-based rules to rule group.

5. Choose **Next**.

6. If you are creating new rules, follow the steps to first create conditions and then rules. For more information, see Working with conditions and Working with Rules. If you are using existing rules, go to the next step.

7. Type a rule group name.

8. Select a rule, and then choose **Add rule**. Repeat to add more rules to the rule group.

9. A rule group has two possible actions: **Block** and **Count**. If you want to test the rule group, set the action to **Count**. This action overrides any *block* action specified by individual rules contained in the group. That is, if the rule group's action is set to **Count**, requests are only counted and not blocked. Conversely, if you set the rule group's action to **Block**, actions of the individual rules in the group are used. For each rule, select the appropriate option.

10. Choose **Create**.

# Adding and Deleting Rules from a Rule Group

You can add or delete rules in a rule group.

Deleting a rule from the rule group does not delete the rule itself. It only removes the rule from the rule group.

**To add or delete rules in a rule group (console)**

1. Sign in to the AWS Management Console using the Firewall Manager administrator account that you set up in the prerequisites, and then open the Firewall Manager console at https://console/.aws/.amazon/ .com/waf/fms/. **Note**
   For information about setting up a Firewall Manager administrator account, see Step 2: Set the AWS Firewall Manager Administrator Account.

2. In the navigation pane, choose **Rule groups**.

3. Choose the rule group that you want to edit.

4. Choose **Edit rule group**.

5. To add rules, perform the following steps:

   1. Select a rule, and then choose **Add another rule**. Repeat to add more rules to the rule group. **Note** You cannot add rate-based rules to rule group.

   2. Choose **Update**.

6. To delete rules, perform the following steps:

   1. Choose the **X** next to the rule to delete. Repeat to delete more rules from the rule group.

   2. Choose **Update**.

# Working with AWS Firewall Manager Policies

An AWS Firewall Manager policy contains the rule group that you want to apply to your resources. A rule group is a set of rules, and each rule includes conditions that you specify. You can apply only one rule group to a policy, but you can apply the same rule group to multiple policies.

Firewall Manager applies the policy to resource types that you specify (such as CloudFront distributions or Application Load Balancers) in all accounts within your organization in AWS Organizations. You cannot exclude individual accounts from the policy.

If you add a new account to your organization, Firewall Manager automatically applies the policy to the specified resources in that account.

**Topics**

- Creating an AWS Firewall Manager Policy
- Deleting an AWS Firewall Manager Policy

# Creating an AWS Firewall Manager Policy

When you create an AWS Firewall Manager policy, you specify which rule group to add to the policy.

**To create a Firewall Manager policy (console)**

1. Sign in to the AWS Management Console using the Firewall Manager administrator account that you set up in the prerequisites, and then open the Firewall Manager console at https://console/.aws/.amazon/ .com/waf/fms/. **Note**
   For information about setting up a Firewall Manager administrator account, see Step 2: Set the AWS Firewall Manager Administrator Account.

2. In the navigation pane, choose **Security policies**.

3. Choose **Create policy**.

4. If you already created the rule group that you want to add to the policy, choose **Create an AWS Firewall Manager policy and add existing rule groups**. If you want to create a new rule group, choose **Create an AWS Firewall Manager policy and add a new rule group**.

5. If you are using an existing rule group, skip this step and go to the next step. If you are creating a rule group, follow the instructions in Creating a Rule Group. After you create the rule group, continue with the following steps.

6. Type a policy name.

7. For **Region**, choose an AWS Region.

8. Select a rule group to add, and then choose **Add rule group**.

9. A policy has two possible actions: **Action set by rule group** and **Count**. If you want to test the policy and rule group, set the action to **Count**. This action overrides any *block* action specified by the rule group contained in the policy. That is, if the policy's action is set to **Count**, those requests are only counted and not blocked. Conversely, if you set the policy's action to **Action set by rule group**, actions of the rule group in the policy are used. Choose the appropriate action.

10. Choose **Next**.

11. Choose the type of resource that you want to protect.

    You can select only one type of resource per policy.

12. If you want to protect only resources with specific tags, or alternatively exclude resources with specific tags, select **Use tags to include/exclude resources**, type the tags and then choose either **Include** or **Exclude**. You can choose only one option.

    If you enter more than one tag (separated by commas), if a resource has any of those tags, it is considered a match.

    For more information about tags, see Working with Tag Editor .

13. If you want to automatically apply the policy to existing resources, choose **Create and apply this policy to existing and new resources**.

    This option creates a web ACL in each account within an organization in AWS Organizations and associates the web ACL with the resources in the accounts. This option also applies the policy to all new resources that match the preceding criteria (resource type and tags). Alternatively, if you choose **Create policy but do not apply the policy to existing or new resources**, Firewall Manager creates a web ACL in each account within the organization, but doesn't apply the web ACL to any resources. You must apply the policy to resources later. Choose the appropriate option.

14. Choose **Next**.

15. Review the new policy. To make any changes, choose **Edit**. When you are satisfied with the policy, choose **Create and apply policy. Note**
Firewall Manager applies a policy to all accounts in your organization in AWS Organizations. You can't include or exclude individual accounts. If you add a new account to the organization, Firewall Manager automatically applies the policy to that account.

# Deleting an AWS Firewall Manager Policy

You can delete a Firewall Manager policy by performing the following steps.

**To delete a policy (console)**

1. In the navigation pane, choose **Security policies**.

2. Choose the circle next to the policy that you want to delete.

3. Choose **Delete**.

# Viewing Resource Compliance with a Policy

You can check to see what resources an AWS Firewall Manager policy is being applied to.

**To check what resources a Firewall Manager policy is being applied to (console)**

1. Sign in to the AWS Management Console using the AWS Firewall Manager administrator account that you set up in the prerequisites, and then open the Firewall Manager console at https://console/.aws/.amazon/.com/waf/fms/. **Note**
   For information about setting up a Firewall Manager administrator account, see Step 2: Set the AWS Firewall Manager Administrator Account.

2. In the navigation pane, choose **Security policies**.

3. Choose a policy. Firewall Manager lists each account in the organization and shows the status. A **Compliant** status indicates that the policy has been applied to all applicable resources in the account. A **Noncompliant** status indicates that the policy is not applied to all resources in the account.

4. Choose an account. Firewall Manager lists each resource in the account and shows the status. A **Compliant** status indicates that the policy is applied to the resource. A **Noncompliant** status indicates that the policy is not applied to the resource. Firewall Manager lists up to 100 noncompliant resources.

# Designating a Different Account as the AWS Firewall Manager Administrator Account

To use AWS Firewall Manager, you must log in to the console with a Firewall Manager administrator account. You can designate only one account in an organization as a Firewall Manager administrator account. It can be an AWS Organizations master account or a member account. To set up an administrator account for the first time, see Step 2: Set the AWS Firewall Manager Administrator Account.

If you designate an account as an administrator account, and you later want to designate a different account as the administrator account, perform the following procedure.

**Important**
To designate a different account, you first must revoke administrator privileges from the current administrator account. When you revoke the privileges, all Firewall Manager policies created by that account are deleted. You then must sign into Firewall Manager with the AWS Organizations master account to designate a new administrator account.

**To designate a different account as the Firewall Manager administrator account (console)**

1. Sign in to the AWS Management Console using the current Firewall Manager administrator account, and then open the Firewall Manager console at https://console/.aws/.amazon/.com/waf/fms/.

2. In the navigation pane, choose **Settings**.

3. Choose **Revoke administrator account. Important**
   When you revoke administrator privileges from the current administrator account, all Firewall Manager policies created by that account are deleted.

4. Sign out of the AWS Management console.

5. Sign in to the AWS Management Console using your AWS Organizations master account. You can sign in using your root user credentials for the account (not recommended) or you can sign in using an IAM user or IAM role within the account that has equivalent permissions.

6. Open the Firewall Manager console at https://console/.aws/.amazon/.com/waf/fms/.

7. Choose **Get started**.

8. Type an account ID to associate with Firewall Manager. This account will be the new Firewall Manager administrator account. It can be the master account that you are signed in with or it can be a member account in your organization. If the account ID that you type is a member account and not the master account, Firewall Manager sets the appropriate permissions for the member account. **Note**
   The account is given permission to create and manage AWS WAF rules across all accounts within the organization.

9. Choose **Set administrator**.

# AWS Shield

AWS provides AWS Shield Standard and AWS Shield Advanced for protection against DDoS attacks. AWS Shield Standard is automatically included at no extra cost beyond what you already pay for AWS WAF and your other AWS services. For added protection against DDoS attacks, AWS offers AWS Shield Advanced. AWS Shield Advanced provides expanded DDoS attack protection for your Amazon EC2 instances, Elastic Load Balancing load balancers, CloudFront distributions, and Route 53 hosted zones.

**Topics**

- How AWS Shield Works
- Example AWS Shield Advanced Use Cases
- AWS Shield Advanced Pricing
- Getting Started with AWS Shield Advanced
- Add AWS Shield Advanced Protection to more AWS Resources
- Removing AWS Shield Advanced from an AWS Resource
- Editing AWS Shield Advanced Settings
- AWS Shield Advanced: Requesting a Credit
- AWS Shield Advanced Limits

# How AWS Shield Works

A distributed denial of service (DDoS) attack is an attack in which multiple compromised systems attempt to flood a target, such as a network or web application, with traffic. A DDoS attack can prevent legitimate users from accessing a service and can cause the system to crash due to the overwhelming traffic volume.

AWS provides two levels of protection against DDoS attacks: AWS Shield Standard and AWS Shield Advanced.

## AWS Shield Standard

All AWS customers benefit from the automatic protections of AWS Shield Standard, at no additional charge. AWS Shield Standard defends against most common, frequently occurring network and transport layer DDoS attacks that target your web site or applications. While AWS Shield Standard helps protect all AWS customers, you get particular benefit if you are using Amazon CloudFront and Amazon Route 53. These services receive comprehensive availability protection against all known infrastructure (Layer 3 and 4) attacks.

## AWS Shield Advanced

For higher levels of protection against attacks targeting your web applications running on Amazon EC2, Elastic Load Balancing (ELB), CloudFront, and Route 53 resources, you can subscribe to AWS Shield Advanced. AWS Shield Advanced provides expanded DDoS attack protection for these resources.

As an example of this added protection, if you use Shield Advanced to protect an Elastic IP address, during an attack Shield Advanced will automatically deploy your network ACLs to the border of the AWS network, which allows Shield Advanced to provide protection against larger DDoS events. Typically, network ACLs are applied near your Amazon EC2 instances within your Amazon VPC. The network ACL can mitigate attacks only as large as your Amazon VPC and instance can handle. For example, if the network interface attached to your Amazon EC2 instance can process up to 10 Gbps, volumes over 10 Gbps will slow down and possibly block traffic to that instance. During an attack, Shield Advanced promotes your network ACL to the AWS border, which can process multiple terabytes of traffic. Your network ACL is able to provide protection for your resource well beyond your network's typical capacity. For more information about network ACLs, see Network ACLs.

As an AWS Shield Advanced customer, you can contact a 24x7 DDoS response team (DRT) for assistance during a DDoS attack. You also have exclusive access to advanced, real-time metrics and reports for extensive visibility into attacks on your AWS resources. With the assistance of the DRT, AWS Shield Advanced includes intelligent DDoS attack detection and mitigation for not only for network layer (layer 3) and transport layer (layer 4) attacks, but also for application layer (layer 7) attacks.

AWS Shield Advanced also offers some cost protection against spikes in your AWS bill that could result from a DDoS attack. This cost protection is provided for your Elastic Load Balancing load balancers, CloudFront distributions, Route 53 hosted zones, and Amazon EC2 instances.

AWS WAF is included with AWS Shield Advanced at no extra cost. For more information about AWS Shield Advanced pricing, see AWS Shield Advanced Pricing.

## Types of DDoS Attacks

AWS Shield Advanced provides expanded protection against many types of attacks. For example:

### User Datagram Protocol (UDP) reflection attacks
An attacker can spoof the source of a request and use UDP to elicit a large response from the server. The extra network traffic directed towards the spoofed, attacked IP address can slow the targeted server and prevent legitimate users from accessing needed resources.

**SYN flood**

The intent of an SYN flood attack is to exhaust the available resources of a system by leaving connections in a half-open state. When a user connects to a TCP service like a web server, the client sends a SYN packet. The server returns an acknowledgment, and the client returns its own acknowledgement, completing the three-way handshake. In an SYN flood, the third acknowledgment is never returned, and the server is left waiting for a response. This can prevent other users from connecting to the server.

**DNS query flood**

In a DNS query flood, an attacker uses multiple DNS queries to exhaust the resources of a DNS server. AWS Shield Advanced can help provide protection against DNS query flood attacks on Route 53 DNS servers.

**HTTP flood/cache-busting (layer 7) attacks**

With an HTTP flood, including GET and POST floods, an attacker sends multiple HTTP requests that appear to be from a real user of the web application. Cache-busting attacks are a type of HTTP flood that uses variations in the HTTP request's query string that prevent use of edge-located cached content and forces the content to be served from the origin web server, causing additional and potentially damaging strain on the origin web server.

## About the AWS DDoS Response Team (DRT)

With AWS Shield Advanced, complex DDoS events can be escalated to the AWS DDoS Response team (DRT), which has deep experience in protecting AWS, Amazon.com, and its subsidiaries.

For layer 3 and layer 4 attacks, AWS provides automatic attack detection and proactively applies mitigations on your behalf. For layer 7 DDoS attacks, AWS attempts to detect and notify AWS Shield Advanced customers through CloudWatch alarms, but does not apply mitigations proactively. This is to avoid inadvertently dropping valid user traffic.

You can also contact the DRT before or during a possible attack to develop and deploy custom mitigations. For example, if you are running a web application and only need ports 80 and 443 open, you can work with the DRT to pre-configure an ACL to only "Allow" ports 80 and 443.

AWS Shield Advanced customers have two options to mitigate layer 7 attacks:

- **Provide your own mitigations:** AWS WAF is included with AWS Shield Advanced at no extra cost. You can create your own AWS WAF rules to mitigate the DDoS attacks. AWS provides preconfigured templates to get you started quickly. The templates include a set of AWS WAF rules that are designed to block common web-based attacks. You can customize the templates to fit your business needs. For more information, see AWS WAF Security Automations.

  In this case, the DRT is not involved. You can, however, engage the DRT for guidance on implementing best practices such as AWS WAF common protections.

- **Engage the DRT:** If you want additional support in addressing an attack, you can contact the AWS Support Center. Critical and urgent cases are routed directly to DDoS experts. With AWS Shield Advanced, complex cases can be escalated to the DRT, which has deep experience in protecting AWS, Amazon.com, and its subsidiaries. If you are an AWS Shield Advanced customer, you also can request special handling instructions for high severity cases.

  The response time for your case depends on the severity that you select and the response times, which are documented on the AWS Support Plans page.

  The DRT helps you triage the DDoS attack to identify attack signatures and patterns. With your consent, the DRT creates and deploys AWS WAF rules to mitigate the attack.

When AWS Shield Advanced detects a large layer 7 attack against one of your applications, the DRT might proactively contact you. The DRT triages the DDoS incident and creates AWS WAF mitigations. The DRT then contacts you for consent to apply the AWS WAF rules.

**Important**

The DRT can help you to analyze suspicious activity and assist you to mitigate the issue. This mitigation often requires the DRT to create or update web access control lists (web ACLs) in your account. However, they need your permission to do so. We recommend that as part of enabling AWS Shield Advanced, you follow the steps in Step 3: (Optional) Authorize the DDoS Response Team to proactively provide the DRT with the needed permissions. Providing permission ahead of time helps prevent any delays in the event of an actual attack.

## Help Me Choose a Protection Plan

In many cases, AWS Shield Standard protection is sufficient for your needs. AWS services and technologies are built to provide resilience in the face of the most common DDoS attacks. Supplementing this built-in protection with AWS WAF and a combination of other AWS services as a defense-in-depth strategy typically provides adequate attack protection and mitigation. Further, if you have the technical expertise and want full control over monitoring for and mitigating layer 7 attacks, AWS Shield Standard is likely the appropriate choice. For additional resources to help you design your own DDoS protection, see our Tutorials.

If your business or industry is a likely target of DDoS attacks, or if you prefer to let AWS handle the majority of DDoS protection and mitigation responsibilities for layer 3, layer 4, and layer 7 attacks, AWS Shield Advanced might be the best choice. AWS Shield Advanced not only provides layer 3 and layer 4 protection and mitigation, but also includes AWS WAF at no extra charge and DRT assistance for layer 7 attacks. If you use AWS WAF and AWS Shield Standard, you must design your own layer 7 protection and mitigation processes.

AWS Shield Advanced customers also benefit from detailed information about DDoS attacks against their AWS resources. While AWS Shield Standard provides automatic protection for the most common layer 3 and layer 4 attacks, visibility into the details of those attacks is limited. AWS Shield Advanced provides you with extensive data about the details of both layer 3, layer 4, and layer 7 DDoS attacks.

AWS Shield Advanced also offers cost protection for DDoS attacks against your AWS resources. This valuable feature helps prevent unexpected spikes in your bill caused by DDoS attacks. If cost predictability is important to you, AWS Shield Advanced can offer that stability.

The following table shows a comparison of AWS Shield Standard and AWS Shield Advanced.

| Feature | AWS Shield Standard | AWS Shield Advanced |
|---|---|---|
| Active Monitoring | | |
| Network flow monitoring | Yes | Yes |
| Automatic always-on detection | Yes | Yes |
| Automated application (layer 7) traffic monitoring | | Yes |
| DDoS Mitigations | | |
| Helps protect against common DDoS attacks, such as SYN flood and UDP reflection attacks | Yes | Yes |
| Access to additional DDoS mitigation capacity, including automatic deployment of network ACLs to the AWS border during an attack | | Yes |
| Custom application layer (layer 7) mitigations | Yes, through user-created AWS WAF ACLs. Incurs standard AWS WAF charges. | Yes, through user-created or DRT-created AWS WAF ACLs. Included as part of the AWS Shield Advanced subscription. |
| Instant rule updates | Yes, through user-created AWS WAF ACLs. Incurs standard AWS WAF charges. | Yes |

| Feature | AWS Shield Standard | AWS Shield Advanced |
| --- | --- | --- |
| AWS WAF for app vulnerability protection | Yes, through user-created AWS WAF ACLs. Incurs standard AWS WAF charges. | Yes |
| Visibility and Reporting | | |
| Layer 3/4 attack notification | | Yes |
| Layer 3/4 attack forensics reports (source IP, attack vector, and more) | | Yes |
| Layer 7 attack notification | Yes, through AWS WAF. Incurs standard AWS WAF charges. | Yes |
| Layer 7 attack forensics reports (Top talkers report, sampled requests, and more) | Yes, through AWS WAF. Incurs standard AWS WAF charges. | Yes |
| Layer 3/4/7 attack historical report | | Yes |
| DDoS Response Team Support | | |
| Incident management during high severity events | | Yes |
| Custom mitigations during attacks | | Yes |
| Post-attack analysis | | Yes |
| Cost Protection (Service credits for DDoS scaling charges) | | |
| Route 53 | | Yes |
| CloudFront | | Yes |
| Elastic Load Balancing (ELB) | | Yes |
| Amazon EC2 | | Yes |

AWS Shield Advanced benefits, including DDoS cost protection, are subject to your fulfillment of the 1-year subscription commitment.

**Note**
Although both AWS Shield Standard and AWS Shield Advanced provide significant protection against DDoS attacks, we recommend that you also use Amazon CloudWatch and AWS CloudTrail to monitor all of your AWS services. For information about monitoring AWS WAF by using CloudWatch and CloudTrail, see Monitoring AWS WAF, AWS Firewall Manager, and AWS Shield Advanced and Logging API Calls with AWS CloudTrail.

# Example AWS Shield Advanced Use Cases

You can use Shield Advanced to protect your resources in many types of scenarios. However, in some cases you should use other services or combine other services with Shield Advanced to offer the best protection. Following are examples of how to use Shield Advanced or other AWS services to help protect your resources.

| Goal | Suggested services | Related service documentation |
| --- | --- | --- |
| Protect a web application and RESTful APIs against a DDoS attack | Shield Advanced protecting an Amazon CloudFront distribution and an Application Load Balancer | Amazon Elastic Load Balancing Documentation, Amazon CloudFront Documentation |
| Protect a TCP-based application against a DDoS attack | Shield Advanced protecting a Network Load Balancer attached to an Elastic IP address | Amazon Elastic Load Balancing Documentation |
| Protect a UDP-based game server against a DDoS attack | Shield Advanced protecting an Amazon EC2 instance attached to an Elastic IP address | Amazon Elastic Compute Cloud Documentation |

# AWS Shield Advanced Pricing

## AWS Shield Advanced and AWS Shield Standard Pricing

AWS Shield Standard is included with your AWS services at no additional cost.

AWS Shield Advanced pricing is detailed on the AWS Shield Advanced Pricing page. AWS Shield Advanced does have an additional cost, but AWS Shield Advanced customers do not pay for AWS WAF separately for resources that they protect with AWS Shield Advanced. Protection for those resources is included as part of the AWS Shield Advanced service. Further, AWS Shield Advanced charges do not increase with attack volume. This provides a predictable cost for the extended protection.

The AWS Shield Advanced fee applies for each business that is subscribed to AWS Shield Advanced. If your business has multiple AWS accounts, you pay just one Shield Advanced monthly fee as long as all the AWS accounts are in the same Consolidated Billing account family. Further, you must own all the AWS accounts and resources in the account.

# Getting Started with AWS Shield Advanced

This tutorial shows you how to get started with AWS Shield Advanced. For best results, perform the following steps in sequence.

**Topics**

- Step 1: Activate AWS Shield Advanced
- Step 2: Specify Your Resources to Protect
- Step 3: (Optional) Authorize the DDoS Response Team
- Step 4: Create a DDoS Dashboard in CloudWatch and Set CloudWatch Alarms
- Step 5: Deploy AWS WAF Rules
- Step 6: Monitor the Global Threat Environment Dashboard

# Step 1: Activate AWS Shield Advanced

AWS Shield Advanced provides advanced DDoS detection and mitigation protection for network layer (layer 3), transport layer (layer 4), and application layer (layer 7) attacks.

**Important**
You must activate Shield Advanced for each AWS account that you want to protect. To activate Shield Advanced for multiple accounts, see Activating and Setting Up AWS Shield Advanced for Multiple Accounts.

**To activate and AWS Shield Advanced**

1. Sign in to the AWS Management Console and open the AWS WAF console at https://console.aws.amazon.com/waf/.

2. If this is your first time signing in to the AWS WAF console, choose **Go to AWS Shield Advanced**. Otherwise, in the navigation pane, under **AWS Shield**, choose **Protected resources**.

3. Read each term of the agreement, and then select each check box to indicate that you accept the terms. Before you can continue, you must select all check boxes.

4. Choose **Next. Important**
   By choosing **Next**, you are subscribing to Shield Advanced and activating the service. To unsubscribe, you must contact AWS Support.

You can now go to Step 2: Specify Your Resources to Protect.


## Activating and Setting Up AWS Shield Advanced for Multiple Accounts

You must activate Shield Advanced for each AWS account that you want to protect. To do so, follow the procedure in Step 1: Activate AWS Shield Advanced for each account, each time logging in with a different account.

If you activate Shield Advanced for multiple accounts that are in the same consolidated billing account family, the monthly subscription fee covers all those accounts. You don't pay extra subscription fees for individual accounts. You must own all the AWS accounts and resources in the account.

The first time that you activate Shield Advanced from an account, you are presented with a pricing agreement. The pricing agreement displays in the console each time that you activate Shield Advanced from a different account. The pricing agreement covers all activated accounts in a consolidated billing family, but you must agree to the terms each time that you activate an account.

You can now go to Step 2: Specify Your Resources to Protect.

# Step 2: Specify Your Resources to Protect

After you activate your AWS Shield Advanced subscription, as described in Step 1: Activate AWS Shield Advanced, you specify the resources you want to protect.

**To select the resources to protect with Shield Advanced**

1. Choose the resources to protect. For load balancers or Elastic IP addresses, you also must choose a region.

   You can choose from the drop-down list, or you can type the Amazon Resource Name (ARN) of specific resources to protect. You can choose or type any combination of resource types and resources. If you enter an ARN, the ARN must be in the same account that you are working from.

   Shield Advanced lists a maximum of 100 resources at one time. If you have more than 100 resources, choose **Next** to see the next set.

   If you want to protect an Amazon EC2 instance, you must first associate an Elastic IP address to the instance, and then choose the Elastic IP address as the resource to protect.

   If you choose an Elastic IP address as the resource to protect, Shield Advanced protects whatever resource is associated with that Elastic IP address, either an Amazon EC2 instance or an Elastic Load Balancing load balancer. Shield Advanced automatically identifies the type of resource that is associated with the Elastic IP address and applies the appropriate mitigations for that resource, including configuring network ACLs that are specific to that Elastic IP address. For more information about using Elastic IP addresses with your AWS resources, see the appropriate guide: Amazon Elastic Compute Cloud Documentation or Elastic Load Balancing Documentation.

   Shield Advanced does not support EC2-Classic. **Important**
   You can continue from this step without choosing any resources. However, if you do so, you must add resources later as described in Add AWS Shield Advanced Protection to more AWS Resources. Shield Advanced doesn't protect resources automatically; you must specify the resources that you want to protect.

2. Choose **Next**.

You can now go to Step 3: (Optional) Authorize the DDoS Response Team

# Step 3: (Optional) Authorize the DDoS Response Team

One of the benefits of AWS Shield Advanced is support from the DDoS response team (DRT). When you experience a potential DDoS attack, you can contact the AWS Support Center. If necessary, the Support Center escalates your issue to the DRT. The DRT can help you analyze the suspicious activity and assist you in mitigating the issue. This mitigation often involves creating or updating AWS WAF rules and web access control lists (web ACLs) in your account. The DRT can inspect your AWS WAF configuration and create or update AWS WAF rules and web ACLs for you, but the team needs your authorization to do so. We recommend that as part of setting up AWS Shield Advanced, you proactively provide the DRT with the needed authorization. Providing authorization ahead of time helps prevent mitigation delays in the event of an actual attack.

If you do *not* want to authorize the DRT to mitigate potential attacks on your behalf, choose **Do not grant the DRT access to my account** and then **Finish**. Otherwise, continue with the following steps.

**Note**
To use the services of the DRT, you must be subscribed to the Business Support plan or the Enterprise Support plan.

**To authorize the DRT to mitigate potential attacks on your behalf**

1. After you complete Step 1: Activate AWS Shield Advanced, the **Authorize DRT support** page appears. Select either **Create new role for the DRT to access my account** or **Choose an existing role for the DRT to access my account**.

   If you choose to use an existing role, must you must attach the `AWSShieldDRTAccessPolicy` managed policy to the role. For more information, see Attaching and Detaching IAM Policies. If you choose **Create new role for the DRT to access my account**, this policy will be attached to the role automatically.

   If you choose to use an existing role, the role must also trust the service principal `drt.shield.amazonaws.com`. For more information, see IAM JSON Policy Elements: Principal.

   The `AWSShieldDRTAccessPolicy` managed policy gives the DRT full access to only your AWS WAF and Shield resources. The policy enables the DRT to inspect your AWS WAF configuration and create or update AWS WAF rules and web ACLs on your behalf. The DRT takes these actions only if explicitly authorized by you.

2. Complete the necessary information, either the new role name or the existing role name.

3. (Optional) Choose **Authorize the DRT to access your flow logs stored in Amazon S3 buckets**, and then type the name of your Amazon S3 bucket where those logs are stored. Choose **Add bucket**. Repeat as necessary, adding more buckets, to a maximum of 10.

4. We send notifications of possible DDoS activity to the email address that is associated with your account. If you want us to send notifications to additional email addresses, type each address in the box and choose **Add email address**. Repeat as necessary to add more email addresses, to a maximum of 10.

5. Choose **Finish**.

You can change DRT access and permissions at any time by following the instructions in Editing AWS Shield Advanced Settings.

After you authorize the DRT to act on your behalf, we recommend that you follow the instructions in Step 4: Create a DDoS Dashboard in CloudWatch and Set CloudWatch Alarms .

163

## Step 4: Create a DDoS Dashboard in CloudWatch and Set CloudWatch Alarms

You can monitor potential DDoS activity using CloudWatch, which collects and processes raw data from Shield Advanced into readable, near real-time metrics. These statistics are recorded for a period of two weeks, so that you can access historical information and gain a better perspective on how your web application or service is performing. For more information, see What is CloudWatch in the *Amazon CloudWatch User Guide*.

For instructions for creating a CloudWatch dashboard, see Monitoring with Amazon CloudWatch. For information about specific Shield Advanced metrics that you can add to your dashboard, see Shield Advanced Metrics.

After you create your CloudWatch dashboard, deploy AWS WAF rules using one or more of the resources that are described in Step 5: Deploy AWS WAF Rules.

# Step 5: Deploy AWS WAF Rules

Several resources are available to help you quickly deploy AWS WAF rules. Consider taking advantage of one or more of the following offerings when creating your initial set of rules:

**Security automation templates**
AWS provides preconfigured templates that include a set of AWS WAF rules, which you can customize to best fit your needs. These templates are designed to block common web-based attacks such as bad bots, SQL injection, cross-site scripting (XSS), HTTP floods, and known-attacker attacks. In addition to activating Shield Advanced and specifying resources for Shield Advanced protection, you also should use these preconfigured templates. For more information, see AWS WAF Security Automations. AWS WAF is included with Shield Advanced at no additional cost.

**AWS Marketplace rule groups**
AWS WAF provides *AWS Marketplace rule groups* to help you protect your resources. AWS Marketplace rule groups are collections of predefined, ready-to-use rules that are written and updated by AWS and AWS partner companies. For more information, see AWS Marketplace Rule Groups.

**AWS WAF for OWASP Top 10 Web Application Vulnerabilities**
This document outlines how you can use AWS WAF to mitigate the application vulnerabilities that are defined in the Open Web Application Security Project (OWASP) Top 10 list. This list shows the most common categories of application security flaws. For more information, see AWS WAF Security Automations.

As a final step for getting started with Shield Advanced, review the global threat environment dashboard, as described in Step 6: Monitor the Global Threat Environment Dashboard .

# Step 6: Monitor the Global Threat Environment Dashboard

The global threat environment dashboard provides a near real-time summary of the global AWS threat landscape. The threat landscape includes the largest attack, the top attack vectors, and the relative number of significant attacks. To view the history of significant DDoS attacks, you can customize the dashboard for different time durations. For more information, see Monitoring Threats Across AWS.

# Add AWS Shield Advanced Protection to more AWS Resources

As part of enabling Shield Advanced for an account, you choose initial resources to protect. You might want to add protection to more resources. Shield Advanced offers advanced monitoring and protection for up to 100 resources that include any combination of Elastic IP addresses, CloudFront distributions, Amazon Route 53 hosted zones, or Elastic Load Balancing resources. If you want to increase these limits, contact the AWS Support Center.

**Important**
You must complete Step 1: Activate AWS Shield Advanced before you perform this procedure.

**To add protection for an AWS resource**

1. Sign in to the AWS Management Console and open the AWS WAF console at https://console.aws.amazon. com/waf/.

2. Choose **Protected resources**.

3. Choose **Add DDoS protection**.

4. Choose or enter the resource types and resources to protect. For Classic Load Balancer and Application Load Balancer resources, you also must choose a region.

   You can choose from the provided list or enter the Amazon Resource Name (ARN) of specific resources to protect. You can choose or enter any combination of resource types and resources.

   Shield Advanced lists a maximum of 100 resources at one time. If you have more than 100 resources, choose **Next** to see the next set.

   If you want to protect an Amazon EC2 instance, you must first associate an Elastic IP address to the instance, then choose the Elastic IP address as the resource to protect. **Note**
   Shield Advanced does not support EC2-Classic.

5. For **Name**, type a friendly name to help you identify the AWS resources that are protected. For example, **My CloudFront AWS Shield Advanced distributions**.

6. (Optional) For **Web DDoS attack**, select **Enable**. You are prompted to associate an existing web ACL with these resources, or create a web ACL if you don't have one yet.

   You can disable this protection later by following the steps described in Removing AWS Shield Advanced from an AWS Resource.

7. Choose **Add DDoS protection**.

**Note**
If you choose an Elastic IP address as the resource to protect, Shield Advanced will protect whatever resource is associated with that Elastic IP address, either an Amazon EC2 instance or an Elastic Load Balancing load balancer. Shield Advanced automatically identifies the type of resource associated with the Elastic IP address and applies the appropriate mitigations for that resource, including configuring network ACLs specific to that Elastic IP address. For more information on using Elastic IP addresses with your AWS resources, see the appropriate guide: Amazon Elastic Compute Cloud Documentation or Elastic Load Balancing Documentation. Shield Advanced does not support EC2-Classic.

# Removing AWS Shield Advanced from an AWS Resource

You can remove AWS Shield Advanced protection from any of your resources at any time.

**Important**
Deleting a resource will not remove the resource from AWS Shield Advanced. You must also remove the resource from AWS Shield Advanced, as described in this procedure.

**Remove AWS Shield Advanced protection from an AWS resource**

1. Sign in to the AWS Management Console and open the AWS WAF console at https://console.aws.amazon. com/waf/.

2. Choose **Protected resources**.

3. Choose the radio button next to the resource.

4. Choose **Delete protection**.

These steps remove AWS Shield Advanced protection from a specific resource. They do not cancel your AWS Shield Advanced subscription. You will continue to be charged for the service. For more information about your AWS Shield Advanced subscription, contact the AWS Support Center.

# Editing AWS Shield Advanced Settings

You can change AWS Shield Advanced settings, such as adding or removing DDoS response team (DRT) access to your account or adding or removing emergency contact information.

**Edit AWS Shield Advanced settings**

1. Sign in to the AWS Management Console and open the AWS WAF console at https://console.aws.amazon.com/waf/.

2. Choose **Summary** under **AWS Shield** in the navigation pane.

3. Choose **Edit** under either **DDoS response team (DRT) support** or **Emergency contacts**.

4. Make the necessary changes and choose **Save**.

# AWS Shield Advanced: Requesting a Credit

If you are subscribed to AWS Shield Advanced and a DDoS attack results in additional charges for your Amazon CloudFront, Elastic Load Balancing, Route 53 or Amazon EC2 services, you can apply for a credit for the charges by submitting a billing case through the AWS Support Center.

If the AWS Shield Advanced team determines that the incident is a valid DDoS attack and that the underlying services scaled to absorb the attack, AWS provides account credit for charges incurred due to the attack. For example, if your legitimate CloudFront data transfer usage during the attack period was 20 GB, but due to the attack you incurred charges for 200 GB of incremental data transfer, AWS provides credit to offset the incremental data transfer charges. AWS automatically applies all credits toward your future monthly bills. Credits are applied towards AWS Shield and cannot be used for payment for other AWS services. Credits are valid for 12 months.

**Important**

To be eligible for a credit, AWS must receive your credit request by the end of the second billing cycle after the incident occurred.

To request your credit, submit a billing query to the AWS Support Center that contains the following information:

- The words "DDoS Concession" in the subject line
- The dates and times of each incident interruption that you are claiming
- The AWS services (Amazon CloudFront, Elastic Load Balancing, Route 53, Amazon EC2) and specific resources that were affected by the DDoS activity

# AWS Shield Advanced Limits

AWS Shield Advanced offers advanced monitoring and protection for Elastic IP addresses, CloudFront distributions, Route 53 hosted zones, or Elastic Load Balancing load balancers. You can monitor and protect up to 100 of each of these resource types per account. If you want to increase these limits, contact the AWS Support Center.

# Monitoring AWS WAF, AWS Firewall Manager, and AWS Shield Advanced

Monitoring is an important part of maintaining the reliability, availability, and performance of AWS WAF and for identifying possible DDoS attacks using AWS Shield. As you start monitoring AWS WAF and AWS Shield, you should create a monitoring plan that includes answers to the following questions:

- What are your monitoring goals?
- What resources will you monitor?
- How often will you monitor these resources?
- What monitoring tools will you use?
- Who will perform the monitoring tasks?
- Who should be notified when something goes wrong?

The next step is to establish a baseline for normal performance in your environment, by measuring performance at various times and under different load conditions. As you monitor AWS WAF and related services, store historical monitoring data so that you can compare it with current performance data, identify normal performance patterns and performance anomalies, and devise methods to address issues.

For AWS WAF, you should monitor the following items at a minimum to establish a baseline:

- The number of allowed web requests
- The number of blocked web requests

**Topics**

- Monitoring Tools
- Monitoring with Amazon CloudWatch
- Logging API Calls with AWS CloudTrail

# Monitoring Tools

AWS provides various tools that you can use to monitor AWS WAF and AWS Shield. You can configure some of these tools to do the monitoring for you, while some of the tools require manual intervention. We recommend that you automate monitoring tasks as much as possible.

## Automated Monitoring Tools

You can use the following automated monitoring tools to watch AWS WAF and AWS Shield Advanced and report when something is wrong:

- **Amazon CloudWatch Alarms** – Watch a single metric over a time period that you specify, and perform one or more actions based on the value of the metric relative to a given threshold over a number of time periods. The action is a notification sent to an Amazon Simple Notification Service (Amazon SNS) topic or Amazon EC2 Auto Scaling policy. CloudWatch alarms do not invoke actions simply because they are in a particular state; the state must have changed and been maintained for a specified number of periods. For more information, see Monitoring with Amazon CloudWatch.

  Not only can you use CloudWatch to monitor AWS WAF and Shield Advanced metrics as described in Monitoring with Amazon CloudWatch, you also should use CloudWatch to monitor activity for you Elastic Load Balancing resources and Amazon CloudFront distributions. For more information, see CloudWatch Metrics for Your Application Load Balancer and Monitoring CloudFront Activity Using CloudWatch.

- **Amazon CloudWatch Logs** – Monitor, store, and access your log files from AWS CloudTrail or other sources. For more information, see Monitoring Log Files in the *Amazon CloudWatch User Guide*.

- **Amazon CloudWatch Events** – Match events and route them to one or more target functions or streams to make changes, capture state information, and take corrective action. For more information, see What is Amazon CloudWatch Events in the *Amazon CloudWatch User Guide*.

- **AWS CloudTrail Log Monitoring** – Share log files between accounts, monitor CloudTrail log files in real time by sending them to CloudWatch Logs, write log-processing applications in Java, and validate that your log files have not changed after delivery by CloudTrail. For more information, see Logging API Calls with AWS CloudTrail and Working with CloudTrail Log Files in the *AWS CloudTrail User Guide*.

## Manual Monitoring Tools

Another important part of monitoring AWS WAF and AWS Shield involves manually monitoring those items that the CloudWatch alarms don't cover. You can view the AWS WAF, AWS Shield Advanced, CloudWatch, and other AWS console dashboards to see the state of your AWS environment. We recommend that you also check the log files for your web ACLs and rules.

- View the AWS WAF dashboard:

  - On the **Requests** tab of the AWS WAF **Web ACLs** page, view a graph of total requests and requests that match each rule that you have created. For more information, see Viewing a Sample of the Web Requests That CloudFront or an Application Load Balancer Has Forwarded to AWS WAF.

- View the CloudWatch home page for the following:

  - Current alarms and status
  - Graphs of alarms and resources
  - Service health status

  In addition, you can use CloudWatch to do the following:

  - Create customized dashboards to monitor the services that you care about
  - Graph metric data to troubleshoot issues and discover trends

- Search and browse all of your AWS resource metrics
- Create and edit alarms to be notified of problems

# Monitoring with Amazon CloudWatch

You can monitor web requests and web ACLs and rules using CloudWatch, which collects and processes raw data from AWS WAF into readable, near real-time metrics. These statistics are recorded for a period of two weeks, so that you can access historical information and gain a better perspective on how your web application or service is performing. For more information, see What is CloudWatch in the *Amazon CloudWatch User Guide*.

## Creating CloudWatch Alarms

You can create a CloudWatch alarm that sends an Amazon SNS message when the alarm changes state. An alarm watches a single metric over a time period that you specify, and performs one or more actions based on the value of the metric relative to a specified threshold over a number of time periods. The action is a notification sent to an Amazon SNS topic or Auto Scaling policy. Alarms invoke actions for sustained state changes only. CloudWatch alarms do not invoke actions simply because they are in a particular state; the state must have changed and been maintained for a specified number of periods.

## AWS WAF and AWS Shield Advanced Metrics and Dimensions

You can use the following procedures to view the metrics for AWS WAF and Shield Advanced.

**Topics**

**To view metrics using the CloudWatch console**

Metrics are grouped first by the service namespace, and then by the various dimension combinations within each namespace.

1. Open the CloudWatch console at https://console.aws.amazon.com/cloudwatch/.

2. If necessary, change the region. From the navigation bar, select the region where your AWS resources are located. For more information, see AWS Regions and Endpoints.

   If you want to view AWS WAF metrics for CloudFront, you must choose the US East (N. Virginia) region.

3. In the navigation pane, choose **Metrics**.

4. On the **All metrics** tab, choose the appropriate service.

**To view metrics using the AWS CLI**

- For AWS WAF, at a command prompt use the following command:

```
1. aws cloudwatch list-metrics --namespace "WAF"
```

   For Shield Advanced, at a command prompt use the following command:

```
1. aws cloudwatch list-metrics --namespace "DDoSProtection"
```

## AWS WAF Metrics

The WAF namespace includes the following metrics.

| Metric | Description |
|---|---|
| AllowedRequests | The number of allowed web requests. Reporting criteria: There is a nonzero value Valid statistics: Sum |

| Metric | Description |
| --- | --- |
| BlockedRequests | The number of blocked web requests. Reporting criteria: There is a nonzero value Valid statistics: Sum |
| CountedRequests | The number of counted web requests. Reporting criteria: There is a nonzero value A counted web request is one that matches all of the conditions in a particular rule. Counted web requests are typically used for testing. Valid statistics: Sum |
| PassedRequests | The number of passed requests for a rule group. Reporting criteria: There is a nonzero value Passed requests are requests that did not match any rule contained in the rule group. Valid statistics: Sum |

## AWS WAF Dimensions

AWS WAF for CloudFront can use the following dimension combinations:

- Rule, WebACL
- RuleGroup, WebACL
- Rule, RuleGroup

AWS WAF for Application Load Balancer can use the following dimension combinations:

- Region, Rule, WebACL
- Region, RuleGroup, WebACL
- Region, Rule, RuleGroup

| Dimension | Description |
| --- | --- |
| Rule | One of the following: [See the AWS documentation website for more details] |
| RuleGroup | The metric name of the RuleGroup. |
| WebACL | The metric name of the WebACL. |
| Region | The region of the application load balancer. |

## Shield Advanced Metrics

### AWS Shield Advanced Metrics

AWS Shield Advanced includes the following metrics.

| Metric | Description |
| --- | --- |
| DDoSDetected | Indicates a DDoS event for a particular Amazon Resource Name (ARN). Reporting criteria: Non-zero value indicates a DDoS event. Zero when there is no DDoS event detected. |

| Metric | Description |
|---|---|
| DDoSAttackBitsPerSecond | The number of bytes observed during a DDoS event for a particular Amazon Resource Name (ARN). This metric is only available for layer 3/4 DDoS events. Reporting criteria: Non-zero value during an attack. Zero when there is no attack. Units: Bits |
| DDoSAttackPacketsPerSecond | The number of packets observed during a DDoS event for a particular Amazon Resource Name (ARN). This metric is only available for layer 3/4 DDoS events. Reporting criteria: Non-zero value during an attack. Zero when there is no attack. Units: Packets |
| DDoSAttackRequestsPerSecond | The number of requests observed during a DDoS event for a particular Amazon Resource Name (ARN). This metric is only available for layer 7 DDoS events and will only be reported for the most significant layer 7 events. Reporting criteria: Non-zero value during an attack. Zero when there is no attack. Units: Requests |

AWS Shield Advanced reports metrics to CloudWatch only when an attack on an AWS resource is detected. If there are no attacks for a specified period, AWS Shield Advanced reports zero.

Metrics for global resources, CloudFront and Route 53, are reported in the US East (N. Virginia) Region.

Shield Advanced posts the DDoSDetected metric with no other dimensions. The other metrics include the appropriate AttackVector dimensions:

- UDPTraffic
- UDPFragment
- GenericUDPReflection
- DNSReflection
- NTPReflection
- ChargenReflection
- SSDPReflection
- PortMapper
- RIPReflection
- SNMPReflection
- MSSQLReflection
- NetBIOSReflection
- MemcachedReflection
- SYNFlood
- ACKFlood
- RequestFlood

**Creating AWS Shield Advanced Alarms**

You can use these Shield Advanced metrics for CloudWatch alarms. CloudWatch alarms send notifications or automatically make changes to the resources you are monitoring based on rules that you define.

Detailed instructions for creating a CloudWatch alarm are in the Amazon CloudWatch User Guide. When creating the alarm in the CloudWatch console, after choosing **Create an alarm**, choose **AWSDDOSProtectionMetrics** to use these Shield Advanced metrics. You can then create an alarm based on a specific volume of traffic, or you can trigger the alarm whenever either of the above metrics is greater than zero. Because Shield Advanced metrics are only reported when an attack is detected, the second option would trigger an alarm for any potential attack observed by Shield Advanced.

**Note**
The **AWSDDOSProtectionMetrics** are only available to Shield Advanced customers.

For more information, see What is CloudWatch in the *Amazon CloudWatch User Guide.*

# Logging API Calls with AWS CloudTrail

AWS WAF, AWS Shield Advanced and AWS Firewall Manager are integrated with AWS CloudTrail, a service that provides a record of actions taken by a user, role, or an AWS service. If you create a trail, you can enable continuous delivery of CloudTrail events to an Amazon S3 bucket, Amazon CloudWatch Logs, and Amazon CloudWatch Events. Using the information collected by CloudTrail, you can determine the request that was made to these services, the IP address from which the request was made, who made the request, when it was made, and additional details.

Every event or log entry contains information about who generated the request. The identity information helps you determine the following:

- Whether the request was made with root or IAM user credentials.
- Whether the request was made with temporary security credentials for a role or federated user.
- Whether the request was made by another AWS service.

For more information, see the CloudTrail userIdentity Element.

CloudTrail log files can contain one or more log entries. Each entry lists multiple JSON-formatted events. A log entry represents a single request from any source and includes information about the requested action, the date and time of the action, request parameters, and so on. Log entries are not an ordered stack trace of the public API calls, so they do not appear in any specific order.

You can create a trail and store your log files in your Amazon S3 bucket for as long as you want, and define Amazon S3 lifecycle rules to archive or delete log files automatically. By default, your log files are encrypted with Amazon S3 server-side encryption (SSE).

You can also aggregate log files from multiple AWS regions and multiple AWS accounts into a single Amazon S3 bucket.

To be notified of log file delivery, configure CloudTrail to publish Amazon SNS notifications when new log files are delivered. For more information, see Configuring Amazon SNS Notifications for CloudTrail.

For more information, see Receiving CloudTrail Log Files from Multiple Regions and Receiving CloudTrail Log Files from Multiple Accounts.

To learn more about CloudTrail, including how to configure and enable it, see the AWS CloudTrail User Guide.

## AWS WAF Information in CloudTrail

All AWS WAF actions are logged by CloudTrail and are documented in the AWS WAF API Reference . For example, calls to ListWebACL, UpdateWebACL, and DeleteWebACL generate entries in the CloudTrail log files.

The following example shows a CloudTrail log entry that demonstrates the following actions (see the `eventName` elements):

- `CreateRule`
- `GetRule`
- `UpdateRule`
- `DeleteRule`

```
1  {
2    "Records": [
3      {
4        "eventVersion": "1.03",
5        "userIdentity": {
6          "type": "IAMUser",
7          "principalId": "AIDAIEP4IT4TPDEXAMPLE",
8          "arn": "arn:aws:iam::777777777777:user/nate",
```

```json
        "accountId": "777777777777",
        "accessKeyId": "AKIAIOSFODNN7EXAMPLE",
        "userName": "nate"
      },
      "eventTime": "2016-04-25T21:35:14Z",
      "eventSource": "waf.amazonaws.com",
      "eventName": "CreateRule",
      "awsRegion": "us-west-2",
      "sourceIPAddress": "AWS Internal",
      "userAgent": "console.amazonaws.com",
      "requestParameters": {
        "name": "0923ab32-7229-49f0-a0e3-66c81example",
        "changeToken": "19434322-8685-4ed2-9c5b-9410bexample",
        "metricName": "0923ab32722949f0a0e366c81example"
      },
      "responseElements": {
        "rule": {
          "metricName": "0923ab32722949f0a0e366c81example",
          "ruleId": "12132e64-6750-4725-b714-e7544example",
          "predicates": [

          ],
          "name": "0923ab32-7229-49f0-a0e3-66c81example"
        },
        "changeToken": "19434322-8685-4ed2-9c5b-9410bexample"
      },
      "requestID": "4e6b66f9-d548-11e3-a8a9-73e33example",
      "eventID": "923f4321-d378-4619-9b72-4605bexample",
      "eventType": "AwsApiCall",
      "apiVersion": "2015-08-24",
      "recipientAccountId": "777777777777"
    },
    {
      "eventVersion": "1.03",
      "userIdentity": {
        "type": "IAMUser",
        "principalId": "AIDAIEP4IT4TPDEXAMPLE",
        "arn": "arn:aws:iam::777777777777:user/nate",
        "accountId": "777777777777",
        "accessKeyId": "AKIAIOSFODNN7EXAMPLE",
        "userName": "nate"
      },
      "eventTime": "2016-04-25T21:35:22Z",
      "eventSource": "waf.amazonaws.com",
      "eventName": "GetRule",
      "awsRegion": "us-west-2",
      "sourceIPAddress": "AWS Internal",
      "userAgent": "console.amazonaws.com",
      "requestParameters": {
        "ruleId": "723c2943-82dc-4bc1-a29b-c7d73example"
      },
      "responseElements": null,
      "requestID": "8e4f3211"-d548-11e3-a8a9-73e33example",
      "eventID": "an236542-d1f9-4639-bb3d-8d2bbexample",
```

```
63        "eventType": "AwsApiCall",
64        "apiVersion": "2015-08-24",
65        "recipientAccountId": "777777777777"
66      },
67      {
68        "eventVersion": "1.03",
69        "userIdentity": {
70          "type": "IAMUser",
71          "principalId": "AIDAIEP4IT4TPDEXAMPLE",
72          "arn": "arn:aws:iam::777777777777:user/nate",
73          "accountId": "777777777777",
74          "accessKeyId": "AKIAIOSFODNN7EXAMPLE",
75          "userName": "nate"
76        },
77        "eventTime": "2016-04-25T21:35:13Z",
78        "eventSource": "waf.amazonaws.com",
79        "eventName": "UpdateRule",
80        "awsRegion": "us-west-2",
81        "sourceIPAddress": "AWS Internal",
82        "userAgent": "console.amazonaws.com",
83        "requestParameters": {
84          "ruleId": "7237b123-7903-4d9e-8176-9d71dexample",
85          "changeToken": "32343a11-35e2-4dab-81d8-6d408example",
86          "updates": [
87            {
88              "predicate": {
89                "type": "SizeConstraint",
90                "dataId": "9239c032-bbbe-4b80-909b-782c0example",
91                "negated": false
92              },
93              "action": "INSERT"
94            }
95          ]
96        },
97        "responseElements": {
98          "changeToken": "32343a11-35e2-4dab-81d8-6d408example"
99        },
100       "requestID": "11918283-0b2d-11e6-9ccc-f9921example",
101       "eventID": "00032abc-5bce-4237-a8ee-5f1a9example",
102       "eventType": "AwsApiCall",
103       "apiVersion": "2015-08-24",
104       "recipientAccountId": "777777777777"
105     },
106     {
107       "eventVersion": "1.03",
108       "userIdentity": {
109         "type": "IAMUser",
110         "principalId": "AIDAIEP4IT4TPDEXAMPLE",
111         "arn": "arn:aws:iam::777777777777:user/nate",
112         "accountId": "777777777777",
113         "accessKeyId": "AKIAIOSFODNN7EXAMPLE",
114         "userName": "nate"
115       },
116       "eventTime": "2016-04-25T21:35:28Z",
```

```
117      "eventSource": "waf.amazonaws.com",
118      "eventName": "DeleteRule",
119      "awsRegion": "us-west-2",
120      "sourceIPAddress": "AWS Internal",
121      "userAgent": "console.amazonaws.com",
122      "requestParameters": {
123        "changeToken": "fd232003-62de-4ea3-853d-52932example",
124        "ruleId": "3e3e2d11-fd8b-4333-8b03-1da95example"
125      },
126      "responseElements": {
127        "changeToken": "fd232003-62de-4ea3-853d-52932example"
128      },
129      "requestID": "b23458a1-0b2d-11e6-9ccc-f9928example",
130      "eventID": "a3236565-1a1a-4475-978e-81c12example",
131      "eventType": "AwsApiCall",
132      "apiVersion": "2015-08-24",
133      "recipientAccountId": "777777777777"
134    }
135  ]
136 }
```

## AWS Shield Advanced Information in CloudTrail

AWS Shield Advanced supports logging the following actions as events in CloudTrail log files:

- ListAttacks
- DescribeAttack
- CreateProtection
- DescribeProtection
- DeleteProtection
- ListProtections
- CreateSubscription
- DescribeSubscription
- GetSubscriptionState
- DeleteSubscription

The following example shows a CloudTrail log entry that demonstrates the `DeleteProtection` action.

```
1
2  [
3    {
4      "eventVersion": "1.05",
5      "userIdentity": {
6        "type": "IAMUser",
7        "principalId": "12345678909876554321231",
8        "arn": "arn:aws:iam::123456789012:user/SampleUser",
9        "accountId": "123456789012",
10       "accessKeyId": "1AFGDT647FHU83JHFI81H",
11       "userName": "SampleUser"
12     },
13     "eventTime": "2018-01-10T21:31:14Z",
14     "eventSource": "shield.amazonaws.com",
15     "eventName": "DeleteProtection",
16     "awsRegion": "us-west-2",
17     "sourceIPAddress": "AWS Internal",
```

```
18      "userAgent": "aws-cli/1.14.10 Python/3.6.4 Darwin/16.7.0 botocore/1.8.14",
19      "requestParameters": {
20        "protectionId": "12345678-5104-46eb-bd03-agh4j8rh3b6n"
21      },
22      "responseElements": null,
23      "requestID": "95bc0042-f64d-11e7-abd1-1babdc7aa857",
24      "eventID": "85263bf4-17h4-43bb-b405-fh84jhd8urhg",
25      "eventType": "AwsApiCall",
26      "apiVersion": "AWSShield_20160616",
27      "recipientAccountId": "123456789012"
28    },
29    {
30      "eventVersion": "1.05",
31      "userIdentity": {
32        "type": "IAMUser",
33        "principalId": "123456789098765432123",
34        "arn": "arn:aws:iam::123456789012:user/SampleUser",
35        "accountId": "123456789012",
36        "accessKeyId": "1AFGDT647FHU83JHFI81H",
37        "userName": "SampleUser"
38      },
39      "eventTime": "2018-01-10T21:30:03Z",
40      "eventSource": "shield.amazonaws.com",
41      "eventName": "ListProtections",
42      "awsRegion": "us-west-2",
43      "sourceIPAddress": "AWS Internal",
44      "userAgent": "aws-cli/1.14.10 Python/3.6.4 Darwin/16.7.0 botocore/1.8.14",
45      "requestParameters": null,
46      "responseElements": null,
47      "requestID": "6accca40-f64d-11e7-abd1-1bjfi8urhj47",
48      "eventID": "ac0570bd-8dbc-41ac-a2c2-987j90j3h78f",
49      "eventType": "AwsApiCall",
50      "apiVersion": "AWSShield_20160616",
51      "recipientAccountId": "123456789012"
52    }
53  ]
```

## AWS Firewall Manager Information in CloudTrail

AWS Firewall Manager supports logging the following actions as events in CloudTrail log files:

- AssociateAdminAccount
- DeleteNotificationChannel
- DeletePolicy
- DisassociateAdminAccount
- PutNotificationChannel
- PutPolicy
- GetAdminAccount
- GetComplianceDetail
- GetNotificationChannel
- GetPolicy
- ListComplianceStatus
- ListPolicies

The following example shows a CloudTrail log entry that demonstrates the `GetAdminAccount` action.

```
1   {
2           "eventVersion": "1.05",
3           "userIdentity": {
4                   "type": "AssumedRole",
5                   "principalId": "1234567890987654321231",
6                   "arn": "arn:aws:sts::123456789012:assumed-role/Admin/SampleUser
                        ",
7                   "accountId": "123456789012",
8                   "accessKeyId": "1AFGDT647FHU83JHFI81H",
9                   "sessionContext": {
10                          "attributes": {
11                                  "mfaAuthenticated": "false",
12                                  "creationDate": "2018-04-14T02
                                        :51:50Z"
13                          },
14                          "sessionIssuer": {
15                                  "type": "Role",
16                                  "principalId":
                                        "1234567890987654321231",
17                                  "arn": "arn:aws:iam
                                        ::123456789012:role/Admin",
18                                  "accountId": "123456789012",
19                                  "userName": "Admin"
20                          }
21                  }
22          },
23          "eventTime": "2018-04-14T03:12:35Z",
24          "eventSource": "fms.amazonaws.com",
25          "eventName": "GetAdminAccount",
26          "awsRegion": "us-east-1",
27          "sourceIPAddress": "72.21.198.65",
28          "userAgent": "console.amazonaws.com",
29          "requestParameters": null,
30          "responseElements": null,
31          "requestID": "ae244f41-3f91-11e8-787b-dfaafef95fc1",
32          "eventID": "5769af1e-14b1-4bd1-ba75-f023981d0a4a",
33          "eventType": "AwsApiCall",
34          "apiVersion": "2018-01-01",
35          "recipientAccountId": "123456789012"
36  }
```

# Responding to DDoS Attacks

Layer 3 and layer 4 attacks are addressed automatically by AWS. If you use Shield Advanced to protect your Amazon EC2 instances, during an attack Shield Advanced will automatically deploy your Amazon VPC network ACLs to the border of the AWS network, which allows Shield Advanced to provide protection against larger DDoS events. For more information about network ACLs, see Network ACLs.

If DDoS alarms in CloudWatch indicate a possible layer 7 attack, you have two options:

- Investigate and mitigate the attack on your own: If you determine that activity represents a DDoS attack, you can create your own AWS WAF rules to mitigate the attack. AWS WAF is included with AWS Shield Advanced at no additional cost. AWS provides preconfigured templates to get you started quickly. The templates include a set of AWS WAF rules, which are designed to block common web-based attacks. You can customize the rules to fit your business needs. For more information, see AWS WAF Security Automations and Creating a Web ACL.

- If you are an AWS Shield Advanced customer, you also have the option of contacting the AWS Support Center: If you want assistance in applying mitigations, you can contact the AWS Support Center. Critical and urgent cases are routed directly to DDoS experts. With AWS Shield Advanced, complex cases can be escalated to the DRT, which has deep experience in protecting AWS, Amazon.com, and its subsidiaries.

  To get DRT support, contact the AWS Support Center and explain that you are an AWS Shield Advanced customer experiencing a possible attack. Our representative will direct your call to the appropriate DDoS experts. If you open a case with the AWS Support Center using the **Distributed Denial of Service (DDoS)** service type, you can speak directly with a DDoS expert by chat or telephone. DDoS support engineers can help you identify attacks, recommend improvements to your AWS architecture, and provide guidance in the use of AWS services for DDoS attack mitigation. **Important**
  For layer 7 attacks, the DRT can help you analyze the suspicious activity, and then assist you to mitigate the issue. This mitigation often requires the DRT to create or update AWS WAF web access control lists (web ACLs) in your account. However, they need your permission to do so. We recommend that as part of enabling AWS Shield Advanced, you follow the steps in Step 3: (Optional) Authorize the DDoS Response Team to proactively provide the DRT with the needed permissions. Providing permission ahead of time helps to prevent any delays in the event of an actual attack.

  You can also contact the DRT before or during a possible attack to develop and deploy custom mitigations. For example, if you are running a web application and only need ports 80 and 443 open, you can work with the DRT to pre-configure an ACL to only "Allow" ports 80 and 443.

# Reviewing DDoS Incidents

AWS Shield Advanced provides real-time metrics and reports for extensive visibility into attacks on your AWS resources.

These metrics and reports are available only for AWS Shield Advanced customers. To activate AWS Shield Advanced, see To activate and AWS Shield Advanced.

You can view near real-time metrics about attacks, including:

- Attack type
- Start time
- Duration
- Blocked packet per second
- HTTP request samples

Details are available for active and past incidents that have occurred in the last 12 months.

## Shield Advanced Details Report

Additionally, AWS Shield Advanced gives you insight into your overall traffic at the time of the attack. You can review details about top:

- IPs
- URLs
- Referrers
- ASNs
- Countries
- User Agents

Use this information to create AWS WAF rules to help prevent future attacks. For example, if you see that you have a lot of requests coming from a country that you don't typically do business in, you can create a AWS WAF rule to block requests from that country.

**Note**
You should always test your rules first by initially using `Count` rather than `Block`. Once you are comfortable that the new rule is identifying the correct requests, you can modify your rule to block those requests.

**To review DDoS incidents**

1. Sign in to the AWS Management Console and open the AWS WAF console at https://console.aws.amazon.com/waf/.

2. Choose **Incidents**.

3. Choose the **Incident type** of the attack you want to investigate.

If you determine a possible attack is underway, you can contact the DRT through the AWS Support Center, or attempt to mitigate the attack on your own by creating a new web access control list (web ACL).

**To mitigate a potential DDoS attack**

1. Create conditions in AWS WAF that match the unusual behavior.

2. Add those conditions to one or more AWS WAF rules.

3. Add those rules to a web ACL and configure the web ACL to count the requests that match the rules.

4. Monitor those counts to determine if the source of the requests should be blocked. If the volume of requests continue to be unusually high, change your web ACL to block those requests.

   For more information, see Creating a Web ACL.

AWS provides preconfigured templates to get you started quickly. The templates include a set of AWS WAF rules, which can be customized to best fit your needs, designed to block common web-based attacks. For more information, see AWS WAF Security Automations.

## Monitoring Threats Across AWS

If you are a Shield Advanced customer, in addition to the information provided on the **Incidents** page about attacks on your own resources, you can use the global threat environment dashboard to view trends and metrics about the DDoS threat landscape across Amazon CloudFront, Elastic Load Balancing, and Route 53.

The global threat environment dashboard provides a near real-time summary of the global AWS threat landscape, including the largest attack, the top attack vectors, and the relative number of significant attacks. You can customize the dashboard view for different time durations to see the history of significant DDoS attacks.

**To view the global threat environment dashboard**

1. Sign in to the AWS Management Console and open the AWS WAF console at https://console.aws.amazon. com/waf/.

2. Choose **Global threat environment**.

3. Choose a time period.

You can use the information on the global threat environment dashboard to better understand the threat landscape and help you make decisions to better protect your AWS resources.

# Using the AWS WAF and AWS Shield Advanced API

This section describes how to make requests to the AWS WAF and Shield Advanced API for creating and managing match sets, rules, and web ACLs in AWS WAF as well as your subscription and protections in Shield Advanced. This section will acquaint you with the components of requests, the content of responses, and how to authenticate requests.

**Topics**

- Using the AWS SDKs
- Making HTTPS Requests to AWS WAF or Shield Advanced
- HTTP Responses
- Authenticating Requests

# Using the AWS SDKs

If you use a language that AWS provides an SDK for, use the SDK rather than trying to work your way through the APIs. The SDKs make authentication simpler, integrate easily with your development environment, and provide easy access to AWS WAF and Shield Advanced commands. For more information about the AWS SDKs, see Step 3: Download Tools in the topic Setting Up.

# Making HTTPS Requests to AWS WAF or Shield Advanced

AWS WAF and Shield Advanced requests are HTTPS requests, as defined by RFC 2616. Like any HTTP request, a request to AWS WAF or Shield Advanced contains a request method, a URI, request headers, and a request body. The response contains an HTTP status code, response headers, and sometimes a response body.

## Request URI

The request URI is always a single forward slash, /.

## HTTP Headers

AWS WAF and Shield Advanced require the following information in the header of an HTTP request:

**Host (Required)**
The endpoint that specifies where your resources are created. The various endpoints can be found in AWS Regions and Endpoints. For example, the value of the `Host` header for AWS WAF for a CloudFront distribution is `waf.amazonaws.com:443`.

**x-amz-date or Date (Required)**
The date used to create the signature that is contained in the `Authorization` header. Specify the date in ISO 8601 standard format, in UTC time, as shown in the following example:

```
1 x-amz-date: 20151007T174952Z
```

You must include either `x-amz-date` or `Date`. (Some HTTP client libraries don't let you set the `Date` header). When an `x-amz-date` header is present, AWS WAF ignores any `Date` header when authenticating the request. The time stamp must be within 15 minutes of the AWS system time when the request is received. If it isn't, the request fails with the `RequestExpired` error code to prevent someone else from replaying your requests.

**Authorization (Required)**
The information required for request authentication. For more information about constructing this header, see Authenticating Requests.

**X-Amz-Target (Required)**
A concatenation of `AWSWAF_` or `AWSShield_`, the API version without punctuation, a period (.), and the name of the operation, for example:
`AWSWAF_20150824.CreateWebACL`

**Content-Type (Conditional)**
Specifies that the content type is JSON as well as the version of JSON, as shown in the following example:

```
1 Content-Type: application/x-amz-json-1.1
```

Condition: Required for POST requests.

**Content-Length (Conditional)**
Length of the message (without the headers) according to RFC 2616.
Condition: Required if the request body itself contains information (most toolkits add this header automatically).

The following is an example header for an HTTP request to create a web ACL in AWS WAF:

```
1 POST / HTTP/1.1
2 Host: waf.amazonaws.com:443
3 X-Amz-Date: 20151007T174952Z
4 Authorization: AWS4-HMAC-SHA256
5             Credential=AccessKeyID/20151007/us-east-2/waf/aws4_request,
```

```
6              SignedHeaders=host;x-amz-date;x-amz-target,
7              Signature=145b1567ab3c50d929412f28f52c45dbf1e63ec5c66023d232a539a4afd11fd9
8 X-Amz-Target: AWSWAF_20150824.CreateWebACL
9 Accept: */*
10 Content-Type: application/x-amz-json-1.1; charset=UTF-8
11 Content-Length: 231
12 Connection: Keep-Alive
```

## HTTP Request Body

Many AWS WAF and Shield Advanced API actions require you to include JSON-formatted data in the body of the request.

The following example request uses a simple JSON statement to update an IPSet (known in the console as an IP match condition) to include the IP address 192.0.2.44 (represented in CIDR notation as 192.0.2.44/32):

```
1 POST / HTTP/1.1
2 Host: waf.amazonaws.com:443
3 X-Amz-Date: 20151007T174952Z
4 Authorization: AWS4-HMAC-SHA256
5              Credential=AccessKeyID/20151007/us-east-2/waf/aws4_request,
6              SignedHeaders=host;x-amz-date;x-amz-target,
7              Signature=145b1567ab3c50d929412f28f52c45dbf1e63ec5c66023d232a539a4afd11fd9
8 X-Amz-Target: AWSWAF_20150824.UpdateIPSet
9 Accept: */*
10 Content-Type: application/x-amz-json-1.1; charset=UTF-8
11 Content-Length: 283
12 Connection: Keep-Alive
13
14 {
15    "ChangeToken": "d4c4f53b-9c7e-47ce-9140-0ee5ffffffff",
16    "IPSetId": "69d4d072-170c-463d-ab82-0643ffffffff",
17    "Updates": [
18       {
19          "Action": "INSERT",
20          "IPSetDescriptor": {
21             "Type": "IPV4",
22             "Value": "192.0.2.44/32"
23          }
24       }
25    ]
26 }
```

# HTTP Responses

All AWS WAF and Shield Advanced API actions include JSON-formatted data in the response.

Here are some important headers in the HTTP response and how you should handle them in your application, if applicable:

**HTTP/1.1**
This header is followed by a status code. Status code 200 indicates a successful operation.
Type: String

**x-amzn-RequestId**
A value created by AWS WAF or Shield Advanced that uniquely identifies your request, for example, K2QH8DNOU907N97FNA2GDLL8OBVV4KQNSO5AEMVJF66Q9ASUAAJG. If you have a problem with AWS WAF, AWS can use this value to troubleshoot the problem.
Type: String

**Content-Length**
The length of the response body in bytes.
Type: String

**Date**
The date and time that AWS WAF or Shield Advanced responded, for example, Wed, 07 Oct 2015 12:00:00 GMT.
Type: String

## Error Responses

If a request results in an error, the HTTP response contains the following values:

- A JSON error document as the response body
- Content-Type
- The applicable 3xx, 4xx, or 5xx HTTP status code

The following is an example of a JSON error document:

```
1 HTTP/1.1 400 Bad Request
2 x-amzn-RequestId: b0e91dc8-3807-11e2-83c6-5912bf8ad066
3 x-amzn-ErrorType: ValidationException
4 Content-Type: application/json
5 Content-Length: 125
6 Date: Mon, 26 Nov 2012 20:27:25 GMT
7
8 {"message":"1 validation error detected: Value null at 'TargetString' failed to satisfy
      constraint: Member must not be null"}
```

# Authenticating Requests

If you use a language that AWS provides an SDK for, we recommend that you use the SDK. All the AWS SDKs greatly simplify the process of signing requests and save you a significant amount of time when compared with using the AWS WAF or Shield Advanced API. In addition, the SDKs integrate easily with your development environment and provide easy access to related commands.

AWS WAF and Shield Advanced require that you authenticate every request that you send by signing the request. To sign a request, you calculate a digital signature using a cryptographic hash function, which returns a hash value based on the input. The input includes the text of your request and your secret access key. The hash function returns a hash value that you include in the request as your signature. The signature is part of the `Authorization` header of your request.

After receiving your request, AWS WAF or Shield Advanced recalculates the signature using the same hash function and input that you used to sign the request. If the resulting signature matches the signature in the request, AWS WAF or Shield Advanced processes the request. If not, the request is rejected.

AWS WAF and Shield Advanced supports authentication using AWS Signature Version 4. The process for calculating a signature can be broken into three tasks:

**Task 1: Create a Canonical Request**
Create your HTTP request in canonical format as described in Task 1: Create a Canonical Request For Signature Version 4 in the *Amazon Web Services General Reference*.

**Task 2: Create a String to Sign**
Create a string that you will use as one of the input values to your cryptographic hash function. The string, called the string to sign, is a concatenation of the following values:

- Name of the hash algorithm
- Request date
- Credential scope string
- Canonicalized request from the previous task The credential scope string itself is a concatenation of date, region, and service information.
  For the `X-Amz-Credential` parameter, specify the following:
- The code for the endpoint to which you're sending the request, `us-east-2`
- `waf` for the service abbreviation For example:
  `X-Amz-Credential=AKIAIOSFODNN7EXAMPLE/20130501/us-east-2/waf/aws4_request`

**Task 3: Create a Signature**
Create a signature for your request by using a cryptographic hash function that accepts two input strings:

- Your string to sign, from Task 2.
- A derived key. The derived key is calculated by starting with your secret access key and using the credential scope string to create a series of hash-based message authentication codes (HMACs).

# AWS WAF and AWS Shield Advanced PCI DSS Compliance

AWS WAF and AWS Shield Advanced are Payment Card Industry (PCI) Data Security Standard (DSS) 3.2 compliant services. The PCI Standards Council published PCI DSS version 3.2 in April 2016 as the most updated set of requirements available. PCI DSS 3.2 has revised and clarified the online credit card transaction requirements for encryption, access control, change management, application security, and risk management programs.

For more information about AWS and PCI DSS 3.2 compliance, see AWS Becomes First Cloud Service Provider to Adopt New PCI DSS 3.2 on the AWS Security Blog. For more information about PCI DSS version 3.2, see PCI DSS 3.2: What's New?.

# Resources

The following related resources can help you as you work with this service.

## AWS Resources

Several helpful guides, forums, and other resources are available from Amazon Web Services.

- **AWS WAF Discussion Forum** – A community-based forum for developers to discuss technical questions related to AWS WAF.
- **Shield Advanced Discussion Forum** – A community-based forum for developers to discuss technical questions related to Shield Advanced.
- **AWS WAF product information** – The primary web page for information about AWS WAF, including features, pricing, and more.
- **Shield Advanced product information** – The primary web page for information about Shield Advanced, including features, pricing, and more.
- ** Classes & Workshops** – Links to role-based and specialty courses as well as self-paced labs to help sharpen your AWS skills and gain practical experience.
- ** AWS Developer Tools** – Links to developer tools, SDKs, IDE toolkits, and command line tools for developing and managing AWS applications.
- ** AWS Whitepapers** – Links to a comprehensive list of technical AWS whitepapers, covering topics such as architecture, security, and economics and authored by AWS Solutions Architects or other technical experts.
- ** AWS Support Center** – The hub for creating and managing your AWS Support cases. Also includes links to other helpful resources, such as forums, technical FAQs, service health status, and AWS Trusted Advisor.
- ** AWS Support** – The primary web page for information about AWS Support, a one-on-one, fast-response support channel to help you build and run applications in the cloud.
- ** Contact Us** – A central contact point for inquiries concerning AWS billing, account, events, abuse, and other issues.
- ** AWS Site Terms** – Detailed information about our copyright and trademark; your account, license, and site access; and other topics.

# Document History

| Change | Description | Date |
|---|---|---|
| Support for query parameters in conditions | When creating a condition, you can now search the requests for specific parameters. | June 5, 2018 |
| Shield Advanced Getting Started Wizard | Introduces a new streamlined process for subscribing to AWS Shield Advanced. | June 5, 2018 |
| Expanded allowed CIDR ranges | When creating an IP match condition, AWS WAF now supports IPv4 address ranges: /8 and any range between /16 through /32. | June 5, 2018 |

## Earlier updates

The following table describes important changes in each release of the *AWS WAF Developer Guide*.

| Change | API Version | Description | Release Date |
|---|---|---|---|
| Update | 2016-08-24 | Marketplace rule groups | November, 2017 |
| Update | 2016-08-24 | Shield Advanced support for Elastic IP addresses | November, 2017 |
| Update | 2016-08-24 | Global threat environment dashboard | November, 2017 |
| Update | 2016-08-24 | DDoS-resistant website tutorial | October, 2017 |
| Update | 2016-08-24 | Geo and regex conditions | October, 2017 |
| Update | 2016-08-24 | Rate-based rules | June, 2017 |
| Update | 2016-08-24 | Reorganization | April, 2017 |
| Update | 2016-08-24 | Added information about DDOS protection and support for Application Load Balancers. | November, 2016 |
| Update | 2015-08-24 | Added information about AWS WAF and AWS Shield Advanced PCI DSS Compliance for AWS WAF. | July 25, 2016 |

| Change | API Version | Description | Release Date |
|---|---|---|---|
| New Features | 2015-08-24 | You can now log all your API calls to AWS WAF through AWS CloudTrail, the AWS service that records API calls for your account and delivers log files to your S3 bucket. CloudTrail logs can be used to enable security analysis, track changes to your AWS resources, and aid in compliance auditing. Integrating AWS WAF and Cloud-Trail lets you determine which requests were made to the AWS WAF API, the source IP address from which each request was made, who made the request, when it was made, and more. If you are already using AWS CloudTrail, you will start seeing AWS WAF API calls in your AWS CloudTrail log. If you haven't turned on AWS CloudTrail for your account, you can turn on Cloud-Trail from the AWS Management Console. There is no additional charge for turning on CloudTrail, but standard rates for Amazon S3 and Amazon SNS usage apply. | April 28, 2016 |

| Change | API Version | Description | Release Date |
|---|---|---|---|
| New Features | 2015-08-24 | You can now use AWS WAF to allow, block, or count web requests that appear to contain malicious scripts, known as cross-site scripting or XSS. Attackers sometimes insert malicious scripts into web requests in an effort to exploit vulnerabilities in web applications. For more information, see Working with Cross-site Scripting Match Conditions. | March 29, 2016 |
| New Features | 2015-08-24 | With this release, AWS WAF adds the following features: [See the AWS documentation website for more details] | January 27, 2016 |
| New Feature | 2015-08-24 | You can now use the AWS WAF console to choose the CloudFront distributions that you want to associate a web ACL with. For more information, see Associating or Disassociating a Web ACL and a CloudFront Distribution. | November 16, 2015 |
| Initial Release | 2015-08-24 | This is the first release of the *AWS WAF Developer Guide.* | October 6, 2015 |

# AWS Glossary

For the latest AWS terminology, see the AWS Glossary in the *AWS General Reference*.